THE PARENT'S ROADMAP TO AUTISM

THE PARENT'S ROADMAP TO AUTISM

A FUNCTIONAL MEDICINE APPROACH

DR. EMILY GUTIERREZ, DNP, CPNP, PMHS, IFM-CP

JANA ROSO, MSN, RN, CPNP

THE PARENT'S ROADMAP TO AUTISM

A Functional Medicine Approach

ISBN   978-1-5445-1331-7 *Paperback*
         978-1-5445-1330-0 *Ebook*

LIONCREST
PUBLISHING

We dedicate this book to all of our patients on the autism spectrum and their families. It has been an honor to be alongside you on your journey of healing.

CONTENTS

INTRODUCTION

LOOKING FOR A ROADMAP

Christy's son was diagnosed with autism last year. She and her husband stay up late almost every night researching solutions, and they have already spent most of their savings taking their son to appointments, subjecting him to tests, and trying every supplement they heard good things about. Most of what they've tried only leaves them exhausted and disappointed, because their approach has not been systematic or individualized. At best, the available approaches seem like a waste of time and money; at worst, Christy wonders if they're safe for her son.

Christy and her husband are desperate to find a way to help their child, but they haven't found a treatment that works. They know a little bit about biomedical treatments and functional medicine, and they would like to know more, but they hesitate to set out on another confusing route in this seemingly endless journey.

Christy's story will sound familiar to most readers who have a child who has been given a diagnosis of Autism Spectrum Disorder (ASD). Such families often feel lost and in need of a roadmap.

In our work with autistic children, we have gotten to know many families like this, whether they have already begun a journey with treatment or are just starting out. We've also seen the remarkable transformation that can occur when parents are given the tools to move from feeling overwhelmed to a place of knowledge and empowerment.

Our experience working with families tells us that parents can create the map they need by using functional medicine—a biomedical approach that looks at the whole body and how its systems function and interconnect. No two children with autism start at the same place on the map, of course, and every parent has a different destination in mind, but the functional medicine approach can help any patient progress toward their full capacity.

Clinicians who treat autism often say, "When you've treated one child with autism, you have treated one child with autism." One family's map won't look exactly like another's, but it will help that family move confidently forward. A functional medicine roadmap can give them the tools they need to pursue the most appropriate practitioners, the most useful tests, and the most helpful treatments for their child.

THE EPIDEMIC OF AUTISM

While autism has been around for centuries, Dr. Leo Kanner was the first to describe "autism" in his 1943 paper, "Autistic Disturbances of Affective Contact." Most people today know someone with autism.[1] That wasn't true fifty years ago, but the number of children diagnosed with autism has risen dramatically in recent years. In 2017, the National Center for Health Statistics estimated that 1 in 36 school-aged children was identified with ASD. For boys, that number was 1 in 27.5.[2] The numbers rise every year.

One reason for the rising numbers is that we now recognize that autism is a spectrum disorder. Its symptoms can range from sensory processing disorder (the child who doesn't seem to tolerate socks with seams or avoids foods with certain textures) to severe autism (a child who won't

---

1   Leo Kanner, "Hans Asperger, and the Discovery of Autism," *The Lancet* 386, no. 10001, (October 3, 2015): 1329-20.

2   Benjamin Zablotsky, et al., "Estimated Prevalence of Children with Diagnosed Developmental Disabilities in the United States, 2014-2016," *NCHS Data Brief*, no. 291 (2017).

make eye contact, is severely speech-delayed, bangs his or her head on the wall, and may be aggressive). Many children diagnosed with autism also receive additional diagnoses (known as comorbid conditions), such as Oppositional Defiant Disorder, Obsessive Compulsive Disorder (OCD), or Attention Deficit Hyperactivity Disorder.[3] In fact, there are many conditions that co-occur with autism that are rooted in physiological imbalances in the body. For example, many children with autism also have problems with their gut (such as chronic diarrhea or abdominal pain). These are the kinds of problems functional medicine aims to treat. We're not trying to fix what is wonderful and unique about each autistic child's personality and talents but focusing deeply on their bodies' physical imbalances.

Families that receive an autism diagnosis might feel scared, but having a label for a child's symptoms isn't a bad thing. It can be quite useful because it gives families and clinicians a common vocabulary. Diagnoses are necessary and are often the key to getting children the therapy that they need. A diagnosis can be critical to getting insurance to pay for treatment as well. Having a diagnosis can also be helpful for obtaining the proper accommodations a child might need to succeed in school. In our work, we're not as focused on naming it, though.

---

3   Virginia Chaidez, Robin L. Hansen, Irva Hertz-Picciotto, "Gastrointestinal Problems in Children with Autism, Developmental Delays or Typical Development," *Journal of Autism and Developmental Disorders* 44, issue 5 (May 2014): 1117–1127.

We're much more interested in looking for the underlying imbalance, regardless of what we call it.

ABOUT THE AUTHORS

We came to functional medicine after years working as pediatric nurse practitioners in mainstream medicine. We were both trained at the University of Texas at Austin, and with only four people in our class, it was easy to get to know one another and realize our ideals and philosophies on life aligned well. We both jumped immediately into primary care and started seeing twenty-five to forty patients a day. Our first foray into the world of conventional medicine was disenchanting. We were seeing patients every ten minutes and giving the same diagnosis and treatment to everyone. It felt stressful and, at the same time, became redundant, boring, if you will, and not as fulfilling as we had hoped. Treating chronic conditions was the most frustrating.

We knew there had to be a better way, but in Austin, the alternatives seemed to be limited to rubbing on essential oils and avoiding medication and vaccinations. This kind of alternative approach was different from primary care practice, but not what either of us were looking for.

When Emily began her doctorate studies at Johns Hopkins University, she started working on this question: how can we bridge the gap between what we practice in allopathic medicine and how can we provide evidence-based integrative care? She dove into the scientific literature, studied at the National Institutes of Health, and spoke with the people who regulate supplements. In the process, she discovered a whole new world of information. In school, she wasn't taught about vitamins and nutrients in healthcare, but now Emily was reading studies about how vitamin C is useful to fight the common cold. In school, she only learned about vitamin C deficiency leading to a rare condition called scurvy (discovered in the late 1700s in maritime sailors), certainly not how to apply it to acute illness.

Studying integrative medicine led naturally to the study of functional medicine and a whole cultural shift in Emily's thinking, which she shared with Jana, who was already exploring nutrition as a means to improve her chronic health concerns. Emily conducted research and published in the medical literature on how it is possible for providers to integrate a more holistic approach into their practice, both safely and scientifically. Emily's doctoral presentation proposed a model of allopathic, or mainstream, care that worked within the larger paradigm of functional medicine to create positive outcomes.[4]

---

4   Emily Gutierrez, JoAnne Silbert-Flagg and Sunita Vohra, "Management of Natural Health Products in Pediatrics: A Provider-Focused Quality Improvement Project," *Journal of Pediatric Health Care* 29, no. 2 (March–April 2015): 137–144; Emily Gutierrez, JoAnne Silbert-Flagg and Sunita Vohra, "Natural Health Product Use and Management in Pediatrics: An Integrative Review," *European Journal of Integrative Medicine* 6, no. 2 (April 2014): 226–233.

Excited to get started, we worked with a pediatric neurologist to start an institute to offer comprehensive services to children with autism and other disabilities. In that practice, we were able to offer good diagnostic services but not a lot of treatment options, which was frustrating for us and our patients. We realized the allopathic model was not the type of structure we needed to provide the type of care we were passionate about.

We were discouraged but quite certain we didn't want to go back to the old paradigm of care, so there was only one thing left to do—start an entirely new type of practice. We found a tribe of other physicians and practitioners who were also practicing functional medicine and received support and encouragement that changed our outlook on how we also might be able to make a difference, and that gave us the courage to move forward. We've now been trained by the Institute of Functional Medicine and the Medical Academy of Pediatric Special Needs, and have completed advanced clinical training in the field of genetics and nutrigenomics. The science is always evolving, and we're always learning.

At Neuronutrition Associates, our Austin-based practice specializing in pediatric integrative and functional medicine, we take a functional, or biomedical, approach to treating children on the autism spectrum. In our practice, we have worked with patients from all across the spectrum and have shared in families' triumphs and achievements, even in some of the most severe cases. It's much more satisfying than our earlier work, but our approach does mean we can no longer see thirty patients a day. Our breakthroughs come because we spend ample time focusing on the child's unique biological makeup and seeking the underlying root of the illness, as well as following up with families over time.

In our practice, we take a higher level of responsibility than clinicians who clock in and clock out. We're there for the entire journey. We take patients under our wing and say, "Here we go. We're with you all the way, and we'll do everything we can to make sure everything is going as well as possible."

ASD IS A MEDICAL DISORDER

Many families we see have already pursued the conventional treatments for autism, which are largely behavioral or pharmacological. Autism is considered a neurodevelopmental disorder, and most patients see a neurologist who prescribes medications and behavioral treatments like speech therapy, physical therapy, occupational therapy, or applied behavioral analysis (ABA) therapy because they see autism as a psychological condition.

We believe all of these therapies are important in the

treatment of ASD, but as practitioners of functional medicine, we see autism as more than a behavioral or psychiatric disorder. We don't look at autism as a psychological disease but a physiological imbalance, a medical disorder. Instead of honing in on a diagnosis and giving a medication, biomedical treatments look at how the body functions as a whole and how it can be brought into balance. Often, if we can detect imbalances within the different systems in the body, we can correct those imbalances and improve a child's overall health, which in turn improves their neurodevelopmental progress. Like medical detectives, we're dedicated to finding the bad guys—the sources of imbalance—wherever they lurk.

Functional medicine conceives of the body as a matrix of systems with lots of places for overall balance to be disrupted. But instead of sending the patient to a series of specialists—a neurologist for neurological symptoms, an immunologist for immunity issues, and a gastroenterologist for gastrointestinal problems—we carefully consider how all of those pieces work together, and how one imbalance can lead to a multitude of symptoms in other body systems.

Every patient's body systems are unique, and we treat our patients with this in mind, unlike many conventional physicians who are accustomed to thinking of patients in large groups. Conventional medicine delivers standard care based on what works for a large percentage of patients in a given group, not necessarily based on what's most appropriate for any individual. Standard treatment for autism includes sending the patient to a neurologist and referring them to ABA therapy, so that is what is done. We believe it's crucial to recognize that each patient responds uniquely to treatment, depending on factors like genetics, environment, nutrition, and toxic exposure.

Medicine is shifting from where the "N" (or patient) had to be a very large sample size in the study in order for us to trust the treatment. Now we are approaching the "N of 1" medical era. We are all unique in our environment, our genetics, our emotional/social input, our access to care, and the list goes on. Instead of treating an individual as if they are a large cohort of people, now we are treating the individual in their individual context.[5]

WHAT IS NEURONUTRITION?

Neuronutrition is the nutritional science related to a person's genetic, environmental, and functional nutrient status and its influence on cognitive homeostasis and optimal brain functioning.

5   Nicholas J. Schork, "Personalized Medicine: Time for One-Person Trials," *Nature: International Weekly Journal of Science* 520 (April 29, 2015): 609-611.

Many people wonder, if our approach is so different from the mainstream, do we ever use conventional medicines? Absolutely. If a patient needs treatment for a severe bacterial infection, we will use the most appropriate antibiotic to treat that, and we're glad it's available. But if he or she has anxiety, we wouldn't rush to hand over a Xanax prescription. Instead, we would think about what else is going on in the body; maybe there is a yeast overgrowth or a methylation deficiency we can treat and out the true cause of the problem. Excessive inflammation in the body can impact brain development, and exploring the cause of that inflammation can improve the symptoms of autism.[6]

Some people have heard that functional medicine is a nutritional approach and wonder how a few diet recommendations can change a child's life. Nutrition is a big part of what we do, but people sometimes assume we work *only* with nutrition, when that's not true at all. We want our parents to understand that having a child's nutrition in the optimal place is a critical foundation to build from. However, we also investigate a wide range of underlying issues and offer an equally wide range of treatments.

---

6   Dario Siniscalco et al., "Inflammation and Neuro-Immune Dysregulations in Autism Spectrum Disorders," *Pharmaceuticals* 11, no. 2 (June 2018): 56.

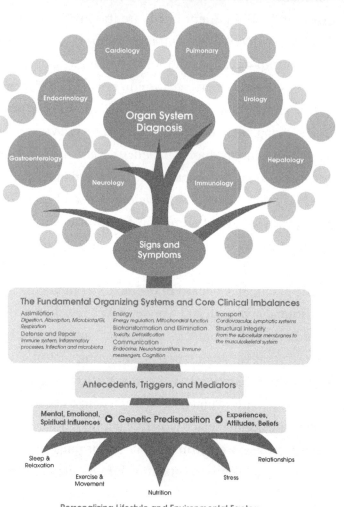

The Functional Medicine Tree

How does our approach look in practice? Let's look at one patient with high-functioning autism who came to us as a teenager. He was on several psychotropic medicines and suffering such severe chronic fatigue that he couldn't even get out of bed. He had such terrible bowel problems, he couldn't leave the house even if he'd had the energy. Our lab work showed this child had hypothyroidism (inadequate and low thyroid hormones) and an immunoglobulin (proteins that help the immune system work optimally) deficiency. He's also severely allergic to coconut, and he was drinking coconut milk every day in an effort to avoid dairy, which was giving him chronic diarrhea. He didn't know any of this. He'd seen neurologists and psychiatrists, but they didn't go down any of these roads.

We have worked with this patient for close to a year now. He's been weaned off the psychotropic medications that weren't controlling his anxiety and depression anyway. He has energy to get up and walk the dog, he's lost fifty pounds, and he's close to finishing his classes for high school. His self-esteem is so much better, he's actually begun developing relationships with girls. He's like a totally different child now, ready to move into adulthood.

At our last check-in with his mother, she said, "You've saved his life, you know?"

In other cases, the benefit of treatment may be incremental and harder for parents to recognize. One patient, a twelve-year-old girl with nonverbal autism, had some serious genetic issues, terrible dysbiosis, and an imbalanced gut. We worked on both areas, and after a few months, she was much healthier. Unfortunately, her parents had completely different perspectives on her progress. Dad was furious. She wasn't talking, so he felt we had failed. Mom, on the other hand, said her daughter was happier than she'd ever been after just two months of treatment. She didn't have diarrhea every day, and she was calmer than they'd ever seen her. From that perspective, treatment was already working, even though we hadn't met the father's goal yet.

We can't promise parents any particular outcome, but we can assure them we will use all the tools we have to improve the status of their child. For some children, that might mean they start saying a few words. For others, it means beginning to meet the same milestones their siblings did. Most parents' biggest hope is that their child will become neurotypical after treatment, but there's a spectrum of recovery too. We aren't going to change someone's personality or make them fit into a certain mold, but we are going to make them the best they can possibly be with the tools we have. Frankly, that's what we want for all children.

FUNCTIONAL MEDICINE AND
BIOMEDICAL TREATMENTS

We use the terms "functional medicine" and "biomedicine" almost interchangeably in this book. Functional medicine is a systems-based way of investigating and understanding the root cause of complex illness pioneered by the world-renowned Cleveland Clinic. It looks at the body in terms of its systems and doesn't treat symptoms in isolation. Biomedical treatments rely on the same systems-based approach.

Many different types of practitioners call themselves functional medicine practitioners, but not all of them have the training necessary to take a truly systems-based approach to health. We have observed it is almost trendy to say you are an integrative or functional practitioner, at least in Austin, Texas. While some practitioners truly are experts, others are tagging on those titles to their practices without the education or experience to back it up. Parents should really understand the training and experience of a practitioner before signing up to be a part of their care.

OUR APPROACH

The biomedical approach to treating autism is becoming more well known as parents share with each other what has worked for their families. About 75 percent of the people who come to us already know a little bit about biomedicine and may have already started doing things like diet changes and supplements. Most of these families have good information, but some have only a partial understanding of the approach and may have absorbed a lot of misinformation in online parenting groups or isolated articles they've read. We listen very respectfully to what they have to say; if they come to us with something we've never heard about, we'll look into it to see if it's true, safe, and useful. Patients usually appreciate our open-mindedness, as it may have been rare in their previous interactions with medical professionals. We believe approaching new ideas with a degree of both skepticism and belief is a healthy balance. Instead of just dismissing a potential truth, it is worth doing due diligence to understand if that truth has validity. If only more practitioners would adopt this ideology, they likely would find some of the best education they will ever receive comes from taking the time to listen, and truly hear, their patients. In contrast, if we had more families open to learning about functional medicine, we would have more children finding paths of new healing.

About 25 percent of our patients come to us with a brand-new diagnosis they're trying to wrap their heads around for the first time. We understand how overwhelming that first visit can be, so we go a little slower and help them choose a starting place rather than trying to address everything at one time. At the same time, we let them know that there's a whole body of knowledge out there showing that helpful treatments for autism do exist. Maybe their doctor wasn't aware of the evidence-based literature supporting these treatments, but we are dedicated to the daily quest of keeping up with the latest research on treatments for autism, and we share that knowledge with our patients. We let them know there's often a knowledge gap between what conventionally trained physicians practice and the latest research. In fact, there's a seventeen-year gap between what we know in the literature and what we practice in medicine.[7]

Closing that gap is challenging, both because doctors become entrenched in the traditional way of practicing medicine and because there is so much new information that it's nearly impossible to keep current. Some practitioners hold off on changing protocols until a major institution like the American Academy of Pediatrics issues clear guidelines, while others look at the evidence, see how people are achieving successful outcomes, and embrace those options. We call the ones who embrace new knowledge "early adopters" and the ones who get stuck "naysayers." We are early adopters. For autism, there aren't a lot of great alternatives to what is commonly practiced in allopathic medicine. Nobody wants to see their child stagnate in treatments that aren't working—especially since the earlier the intervention, the better the outcome. We want to use that window of time wisely.

7   Z.S. Morris, S. Wooding and J. Grant, "The Answer is 17 Years, What is the Question: Understanding Time Lags in Translational Research," *Journal of the Royal Society of Medicine* 104, no. 12 (December 2011): 510–20.

On the other hand, we want parents to know that it's never too late. The human brain is always creating new neuronal networks. Neuroplasticity is the ability of the brain to form and reorganize synaptic connections, especially in response to learning or experience or following injury.[8] This neuroplasticity means we can help our twenty-four-year-old patient with bowel problems and anxiety to take the steps needed to get himself out in the world, and we can help a four-year-old gain new words. Every patient that we have been following has seen improvement in at least one area. The degree of improvement depends on many variables, emotional, physical, and developmental, but everyone can benefit from looking at their health from a functional medicine standpoint.

IN THIS BOOK

Many parents feel frustrated and powerless in their child's recovery, and very alone. They don't have to feel this way. Many others have gone down this road, just like them. That's why we were compelled to write this book: to give families a roadmap to make the journey easier and more successful and to increase parents' awareness of and access to biomedical treatments for ASD patients and families.

---

8   Joyce Shaffer, "Neuroplasticity and Clinical Practice: Building Brain Power for Health," *Frontiers in Psychology*, 7 (2016): 1118.

Most families haven't been made aware that this biomedical approach to treating autism even exists. Mostly, they have listened only to their primary care provider when he or she recommends therapy or medication on a symptom-by-symptom basis. Now, maybe a friend has recommended this new approach, but the pros and cons are unclear. All the new information coming their way can be overwhelming. Stressed parents often don't know how to sort through it all.

Families come to us with a wide range of information and experience. They may belong to online groups dedicated to biomedicine and come to us eager to try everything they've heard of in these communities. Or they may have done some thoughtful research and studied what might be best for their child. Most parents, though, only know we're doing something different.

We want this book to increase awareness and understanding of biomedicine and improve children's access to effective care. We want parents to be able to do some things on their own, but more importantly, we want them to learn how to advocate for their child to receive a different kind of care. In these pages, readers will learn what kinds of questions to ask of providers, what types of tests to request, and what sort of diet and lifestyle changes can make a difference in their child's life.

This book provides readers with a first-of-its-kind roadmap for treating children with ASD through functional medicine. The roadmap we're building is rooted in a profound paradigm shift. We want to help families move from treating the symptoms of a chronic condition to understanding its source. This shift takes us away from reactive medicine and moves us toward proactive, precision medicine.

BEYOND THE BOOK

While our main goal in writing this book is to increase awareness of and access to biomedical treatments for ASD patients and their families, we know one book can't do it all. We also know we can't see enough patients each day to reach all of the families needing help.

To help parents dive deeper into the concepts in this book and learn how to apply them with their children, we are creating online education modules for parents on our website. Also on the site, families will have access to resources like lab tests and supplements (NeuronutritionAssociates.com/store/).

Nobody will be left on their own after reading this book. This isn't the end, but a new beginning.

WHAT THIS BOOK IS AND ISN'T

Please note, we're not claiming to offer a magic cure in these pages. Instead, we are clinicians who are willing to turn over every stone and investigate every potential pathological etiology. We're not trying to call the shots; we want to be our patients'—and our readers'—partners. In the following chapters, we'll help parents fully and comprehensively understand their family's unique story, investigate the cracks in the foundation, and develop ideas for moving forward. This book works like an atlas to orient us for the journey ahead and keep us moving down the roads most likely to reach each family's desired destination.

THE ROADMAP

Many parents, understandably, want to take the direct route to helping their child. They want a map that will take them from point A to point B with no detours. There will be detours, though, and that's not a bad thing. It's actually great because each child is as unique their own path will be.

This journey is a bit like taking an actual road trip. If travelers stick strictly to the map they bought at the beginning of the journey, they'll never know what opportunities they missed by not stopping and looking around. On the other hand, if they proceed with no map at all, they'll probably get lost. All travelers need a roadmap that provides both structure and openness.

This book provides that kind of roadmap for parents of children with autism. Parents want to reach their child's best destination, so they need to identify a starting point and next steps. Reading this book will help them under-stand a whole new approach to treatment, find some things they can try on their own, and help them choose a practitioner who can take them further down the road. When they encounter something out of balance with their child, they want to stop the car, get out, and spend some extra time there. They might make some big gains and then be able to take a shortcut later. We don't know exactly where their roadmap will take them, but we can offer a systematic way of exploring certain roads that can get them closer to their goals.

CHAPTER ONE

START THE GPS

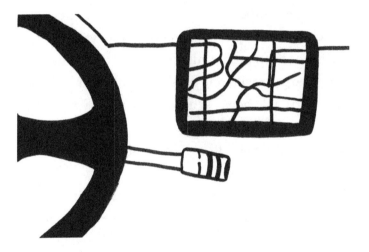

At a patient's first visit to our functional medicine clinic, we get our bearings by exploring three questions: Where have our patients been, what have they tried, and where can we go from here? It's kind of like entering the data for a new trip into a GPS.

It's common for families to come to us feeling like they've reached a dead end. Often, the diagnosis of autism is new. They've just been to the pediatrician, who sent them to a neurologist, and now they have a label (which they never imagined their child would receive and may make them feel despondent now that they have it). Other families may have already tried some of the conventional treatments. They may have been doing ABA therapy for years, for instance, and while their child has made some progress, it's not as much as they'd hoped. Meanwhile, parents often have concerns that they feel the pediatrician has overlooked or that a specialist has failed to treat adequately. For example, the parents of a six-year-old who has never been potty-trained because of chronic diarrhea—the gastroenterologist the family saw merely said he had irritable bowel syndrome of unknown etiology and offered them biologic medications and long-term steroids that came with intolerable side effects.

These families have been around the block, only to find themselves still looking for directions. We can often help them prepare to follow a new route. For the family of the six-year-old introduced above, we can provide reassurance that, despite tests that were negative, there are still answers to find, and we won't stop there. We will look for everything that could be connected to the problem, whether it's parasites, lack of microbial diversity, an infection, or a number of other possibilities. When we start down that road and we show the parents the things we test for, they often express relief that there's more to do. "Wow," they say, "Nobody's ever looked at this. I've never heard the word 'microbiome' before."

Sometimes, the parents already suspect that their child's problems are connected, but they've never had a doctor engage them on those points. A child with chronic eczema, for instance, may not have found relief with the steroid creams her pediatrician recommended. She also has chronic diarrhea. When we start talking to the parent about how the gut and skin are connected, they say, "Why hasn't anyone told me that before? I've been to the dermatologist for eczema, and the gastroenterologist for diarrhea, but nobody talks about the relationship between these things. I've always wondered if they're connected to the autism as well." When we start talking about treating the body as a whole, their eyes light up.

A few parents come to us knowing a little about functional medicine, and they're the most excited by the possibilities. Recently, we saw a child who was two years old and has what's called pervasive developmental disorder. It's not quite autism, but he's nonverbal and has developmental delays. His mother had been looking into functional medicine and knew what she wanted. She sat down in our office, ready to go. We went over some of the things we could look into, and she left feeling hopeful for the first time in a long time.

We're not trying to say that conventional medicine doesn't have its place in treating autism. We absolutely think a lot of these children need to see a neurologist. A study done in 2016 showed the prevalence of epilepsy in autism can be as high as 22 percent.[1] Seeing a neurologist to obtain an EEG and rule out seizures can be an important part of each child's journey. This is only one part of the puzzle, however, one piece of the larger picture.

WHERE HAVE THEY BEEN?

Our first visit with patients is often different from what the patient is used to. Some children have seen several doctors already, and they're quite nervous about what will happen to them. Plus, many patients with autism can get overwhelmed by the sounds and sights in the doctor's office, so instead, we let them get comfortable, play with some toys, and focus on talking to the parents.

We begin by diving into their history, asking the parents for details around their birth, the parents' health, when development started to look different for that child, and

---

1   Patrick F. Bolton, Iris Carcani-Rathwell, Jane Hutton, Sue Goode, Patricia Howlin, and Michael Rutter, "Epilepsy in Autism: Features and Correlates," *British Journal of Psychiatry: The Journal of Mental Science* 198, no. 4 (April 1, 2011): 289–294.

when the parents started getting concerned. "Where have you been?" is often a long story, involving birth history, antibiotic use, environmental exposures, changes in routine, travel, vitamin intake, hospitalizations, illnesses, social dynamics, and more. Do they toss and turn in their sleep? Did they meet their early milestones? Was there a regression, or was the child's development different from the beginning? Was there a traumatic trigger that preceded the symptoms? All of these details give us ideas about what roads to go down looking for answers.

We can do many tests to pin down the hidden triggers of immune problems, but we learn a lot simply by talking with parents and children. As we gather patient history, we ask about the mother's health, diet, and if there were any significant stressors during pregnancy. The first two years are extremely important, so we ask about antibiotic use, diet, if the child was breastfed, and if there were any significant life-altering events. All of these factors play a huge role in the immune system because any setbacks in these areas can result in immune dysfunction.

After that, it's important to look at the physical aspects of the child. Do they have a lot of eczema? Do they have a food intolerance? Allergies? Frequent hives? We also ask what the parent does for a living. Triggers can come from surprising places—we had one patient whose mother flipped houses for a living. She was exposed to a wide array of chemicals, paint, and mold. These toxins can enter the body through the gut and get passed along to offspring.

The first visit is all about trying to understand the child's whole situation, from as far back as we can go.

WHAT HAVE THEY TRIED?

Next, we ask about treatments the family has tried. Have they done ABA therapy? Medications? Supplements? Have they followed a conventional vaccination schedule?

Vaccinations are a tricky subject, and many parents are reluctant to talk about them at all, because their fears have been dismissed in the past. Some families have even been told by their doctor that they are terrible parents and they are thrown out of that particular practice if they refuse to vaccinate on the CDC schedule (even when their previous child had a major reaction to a vaccine that hospitalized them and almost took their life). When they do talk to us, many, many parents tell us their child had multiple ear infections in the first year of life and took antibiotics each time. Then, when he got his twelve-month vaccines, he started regressing. When parents tell us this, we listen to them. There's truth in what they're saying, though we wouldn't say that if they skipped the vaccines they could have avoided the regression. But it's part of the picture, and we want to see the whole picture as clearly as possible.

We want to hear about all the conventional treatments families have tried. Parents sometimes feel that, by coming to us, they're abandoning the things they've tried in the past. That's not the case at all. We assure them that we had the same training as the other practitioners they've seen. We had very similar training to their pediatrician, and we practiced that for many years. We haven't lost our allopathic training; we just have additional knowledge on top of that. We will always collaborate with conventional doctors when needed. We recently saw an eight-year-old boy who was diagnosed with "insufficient sleep syndrome" when he was sleeping fourteen to sixteen hours a day (and still wanted to take daily naps). The sleep doctor and pediatrician had said he was just a child that needed a lot of sleep. When we took a closer look, he had a very high strep infection circulating in his blood. It turns out this immune burden was causing the excessive sleep. We consulted with the ENT doctor, and he had the boy's tonsils removed, and after appropriate use of the right antibiotics, his crippling fatigue improved.

WHERE CAN THEY GO FROM HERE?

We offer parents a whole new map. We show them routes and alternatives they've never seen before. We do a lot of education about what the biomedical approach is and how it can work to take their child to their best possible destination.

Instead of stalling out over an assessment that says the child has a permanent disorder they can label but do little else about, parents can rev up their engines again. Even if we never find the root cause of their child's problems, they can rest easy because we're going to do everything we can to try to understand them. And if there *is* an imbalance that needs correction, we will try everything we can to find it. At the end of the day, the parents know their child is going to be the healthiest child they can possibly be, and they can feel good about that.

A CONTINUUM OF HEALTH

Everything we do in our practice is aimed at restoring balance. Most of the time, this means reducing the burden of stressors in the body. We all have stressors, whether they're environmental, emotional, psychological, or medical. Dr. Martha Herbert, a Harvard-trained pediatric neurologist, says we all exist somewhere on a continuum of health, depending on the loads we're carrying. In her book *The Autism Revolution: Whole Body Strategies for Making Life All It Can Be*, she suggests we can consider a person's health on a continuum from zero to ten, depending on the current load on their system.[2] Everyone falls somewhere on the continuum, whether they have autism, anxiety, or nothing at all. Dr. Herbert moves beyond the

2   Martha Herbert and Karen Weintraub, *The Autism Revolution: Whole-Body Strategies for Making Life All It Can Be* (Ballantine Books: 2012).

conventional thinking about autism, teaching clinicians that they should be looking at how the body is burdened with stressors.

ILLNESS-WELLNESS CONTINUUM

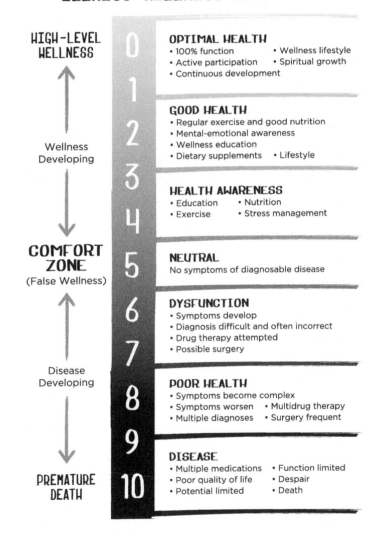

HIGH-LEVEL WELLNESS

↑

Wellness Developing

↓

COMFORT ZONE
(False Wellness)

↑

Disease Developing

↓

PREMATURE DEATH

0

OPTIMAL HEALTH
- 100% function
- Active participation
- Continuous development
- Wellness lifestyle
- Spiritual growth

1

2

GOOD HEALTH
- Regular exercise and good nutrition
- Mental-emotional awareness
- Wellness education
- Dietary supplements
- Lifestyle

3

HEALTH AWARENESS
- Education
- Exercise
- Nutrition
- Stress management

4

5

NEUTRAL
No symptoms of diagnosable disease

6

DYSFUNCTION
- Symptoms develop
- Diagnosis difficult and often incorrect
- Drug therapy attempted
- Possible surgery

7

8

POOR HEALTH
- Symptoms become complex
- Symptoms worsen
- Multiple diagnoses
- Multidrug therapy
- Surgery frequent

9

10

DISEASE
- Multiple medications
- Poor quality of life
- Potential limited
- Function limited
- Despair
- Death

If the patient scored a zero, that would indicate perfect health. His or her system is unburdened by invaders and imbalances. At a ten, they're probably facing a severe threat or the impact of a variety of accumulated threats. That's disease. When we treat chronic disease, we look at the insults the system has suffered and the load it's carrying. Someone who is already at an eight, for example, and gets a nasty case of the flu, could be tipped over to ten in the form of joint pain, chronic fatigue, or some other chronic condition.

We tell all of our families our goal is to push their children back as close to zero as we can. We aim to decrease the body burden to stimulate an increase in resilience, and, hopefully, a reversal of whatever chronic, usually inflammatory, process is happening in the body.

CORE AREAS OF BODY BURDEN

There are five core areas where stress and body burden tend to reveal themselves, in no particular order: gut health, genetics, toxins, immunity, and nutrition. When we first visit with a family, we pull out this list to help them start thinking about all of the systems involved in their child's health. It's not an exhaustive list, but it highlights the major areas we need to investigate. In the following chapters, we'll talk in depth about each area, but a brief introduction to the five core areas offers a solid start in thinking about systems—how one area affects the next and how they all work together.

GUT HEALTH

There's a saying in functional medicine: "When you don't know where to start, start with the gut." The surface area of the gut, if you slice it open, would cover the surface of a tennis court. It's a major part of the highway from the outside environment to the inside of the body. The gut affects our immune systems, our digestion, the way we assimilate nutrients, and more. Children with autism seem to have more gastrointestinal complications, including constipation and diarrhea, which can increase inflammation.[3] Parents can give all the supplements in the world, but if the child has gut inflammation and permeability, it's likely he's not absorbing the nutrients.

We can't recommend supplements without examining the patient's gut health, ruling out leaky gut, and creating a healthier gut environment. Many parents start on the nutrition end. If their child eats meat every day, why is he deficient in vitamin B12? Maybe it's not his diet that's causing the problem. Maybe he has a change in his genetics where the gastric intrinsic factor gene doesn't

---

3   Qinrui Li et al., "The Gut Microbiota and Autism Spectrum Disorders," *Frontiers in Cellular Neuroscience* 11 (2017): 120.

allow him to absorb B12 through digestion. A sublingual or injectable form of B12 might make all the difference.

We'll talk a lot in this book about gut health and how to heal the gut by removing what's bad, replacing what's good, repopulating the useful bacteria, repairing the inflammatory status, and rebalancing the system. Ultimately, we're seeking balance in the gut. More to come on the gut in Chapter 4.

GENETICS

Scientists just mapped the human genome for the first time in 2003.[4] We've known about chromosomal structure and what our DNA looks like ever since Gregory Mendel discovered this in the late 1800s, but we haven't known much about what those genes are doing. It's like we have a massive library available now—we can test chromosomes, depletions, deletions, and duplications to make sure all of the genetic "volumes" are on the shelf—but we haven't actually opened any of those books. Around twenty thousand genes are described in those books, and until we open them and look for misspellings, typos, and missing words, we don't really understand the whole story.

---

4   "The Human Genome Project Completion: Frequently Asked Questions," *NIH National Human Genome Research Institute,* 2003 Release, https://www.genome.gov/11006943/human-genome-project-completion-frequently-asked-questions/.

Science is starting to crack open some of those books, though. One area we're very interested in is single nucleotide polymorphisms (SNPs) in the area of nutrigenomics. Based on the variation in SNPs, we can make specific recommendations that may improve the overall functioning of the body. This goes for everything from how a patient detoxifies, how they methylate, and what influences their mitochondria to work efficiently. We might discover a genetic predisposition for an inflammatory response, for instance, and tailor our treatments to address that. We can do that because genes do change depending on environmental inputs, a science known as epigenetics. Knowing what's there can give us more insight into how to improve the condition we are treating. We'll cover much more on the fascinating world of genetics in Chapter 7.

TOXINS

We are just starting to understand the impact of toxins on our health. A person doesn't have to be exposed to massive amounts of lead to have problems with toxicity. The typical urban environment is laden with toxins, and it's the accumulation of those exposures that can be significantly harmful to the body.

We look at everyday toxins, like the eczema lotion that contains a chemical a patient's body is having to detox from every day, or the plastics in the fidget toys children routinely put in their mouths. In the modern world, it's almost impossible to avoid toxins. Just try to find a crib mattress that's not soaked in flame retardants. It's hard for any parent. For parents of children with autism, it can be even more challenging to find the time, energy, and resources to eliminate these toxins, but it is incredibly important.

Even a child who is at a zero on the health continuum could get pushed up toward a ten pretty quickly in today's world. A child with autism is likely to have a loaded system and have a harder time detoxing, so the environmental factors can be even more potent. We have to create resilience in their systems. We strengthen their immune systems and their ability to detox, so when they do come into contact with toxins, their body is more sophisticated in defense and repair. More on toxins in Chapter 8.

IMMUNITY

The immune system is involved in everything that goes on in the body and can be triggered by a wide range of inputs. We can't talk about immunity without talking about gut health, toxins, and nutrition. Our patients with autism tend to have immune systems that are either overactive or underactive. When most children get a strep infection, for example, they have active immunoglobulins fighting the infection, and we see it reflected in symptoms like a red throat and fever. Often in children with autism, we don't see the usual flags. Instead, we might observe tics, anxiety, or OCD symptoms. Most physicians don't think to test for streptococcal infection in those cases, but in fact, strep could be active in their blood (not even testing positive on a rapid swab in the office), and treating the infection can significantly improve their psychological behavior. We often find that antibiotic, antiviral, or immunoglobulin therapy reduces symptoms that are too often dismissed as behavioral.

Many of our patients have immune systems that have gone into overdrive. Their bodies continue to produce different antibodies toward viruses and bacteria they've been exposed to at some point in their lives. The immune system starts to work overtime to defend them against the attacking army, and it ends up doing more harm in the process. If we address the underlying immune system dysfunction, some of their symptoms improve dramatically. We'll learn a lot more about the immune system in Chapter 5.

NUTRITION

Nutrition is the foundation of good health. Some of our families come in with a clean, anti-inflammatory diet already in place. But the thing about nutrition is that there's not one diet for every person. It depends on where that person is genetically, where their gut health is, and how their immune system responds to certain foods. There is not one prescriptive nutrition for all autism patients, but some we hear a lot about are the Specific Carbohydrate Diet, the ketogenic diet, the low FODMAP diet, as well as gluten-, casein-, and soy-free diets.

Many children with autism eat from what we call "the kid's menu." They seem to prefer a lot of carbs and sugars, and most meals include chicken nuggets, grilled cheese, or French fries. This happens even in families where the rest of the family eats healthy foods.

In our first visit with families, we always address nutritional concerns. We try to get parents thinking about how they might swap out some of the less nutritious options for healthier foods. How can they sneak vegetables into their children's diets? Can they choose organic foods? Can they learn to shop the perimeter of the grocery store and limit access to processed foods? Changing the way their family eats takes a lot of effort, so we provide recipes, resources, and even home visits where a nutritionist can help them take a critical look at their pantry.

We will often conduct blood work and tests that provide a quantitative measurement that pinpoints what's going on in the patient and gives us some data to work with during treatment. It's very satisfying for parents to see their child is receiving and absorbing the right nutrition over time, which ultimately gives them the best foundation to grow and heal from.

We'll dive deeper into nutrition in Chapter 3.

ORIENTING FOR THE TRIP

In our office, we look at each patient's situation as a medical challenge. We're trying to find and address underlying imbalances wherever we find them, be it in one of the five areas above or someplace else. Where a patient in the conventional system gets bumped from one specialist to the next, our patients stay with us through the whole journey. It is a journey. We can't offer one pill for one ill. Autism is complex, and we have to consider a lot of different things at one time.

To make this journey as successful as possible, we've filled our toolbox with the most effective treatments available. These include, but are not limited to, dietary modifications, detox therapies, nutritional supplements, allergy immunotherapies, gut healing protocols, and methylation support to optimize genetic potential. We'll explore all of these and more in the pages ahead, but what parents need to know now is that treatments do exist.

Knowing the basics of the biomedical approach to autism

is the first step. We help families get oriented and set their GPS for an optimal course. To move forward on this journey, let's dig deeper so we know what coordinates to set.

CHAPTER TWO

———

KNOW THE LOCATION

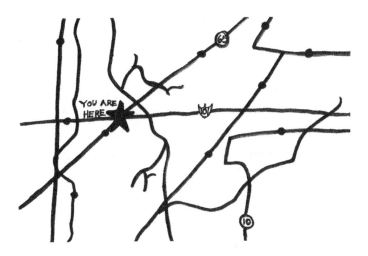

Families begin their functional medicine journeys from different starting points. Maybe they've received a diagnosis for their child but don't know where to turn next. Sometimes, they've exhausted the options conventional medicine offers. Or they've been told to "wait and watch." Some parents know very little about functional medicine, while others have learned a lot about it before they step into our offices.

A lot of parents come to us in a panic. They've heard words like "pervasive developmental disorder" or "autism spectrum disorder," but they don't really know what that means. Now that they have a diagnosis, where, exactly, do they stand? Other parents have a lot of information, but they're in denial. They'll say things like, "I know he is three and doesn't have any words yet, but I was a slow talker too." Not all children who don't speak by three are autistic, but this is a serious issue that needs to be addressed and not dismissed.

Getting oriented means assessing the emotional situation as well as the medical one. Parents need to reach a certain level of acceptance and be willing to address the issues they face, no matter how overwhelming it might seem.

Every child, and every family, is different, but what all families starting this journey have in common is the need to know the lay of the land—where they are right now, what is going on with their child, and what their goals are for the future.

ESTABLISH BEARINGS

In primary care, the standard evaluation process often

begins with the Modified Checklist for Autism in Toddlers, or M-CHAT, a two-page parent report that is given at intervals between sixteen and thirty months. While useful, these questionnaires can miss a lot of things. They're based on CDC guidelines for developmental milestones that suggest babies should hold their heads up or begin talking in certain age ranges. The M-CHAT can help the pediatrician make sure the child is meeting these milestones, but it's not a rigorous test. A recent study, published in September 2017, showed that 23 out of 28 autistic children screened negative on the M-CHAT.[1] This makes us question the accuracy of self-reported questionnaires that don't probe very deeply.

Because the M-CHAT result alone isn't sufficient to diagnose autism, the child often needs to go to the neurologist or developmental pediatrician to undergo additional developmental screenings. All children suspected of having autism are not required to undergo the various types of neurodevelopmental testing if the diagnosis is clear; however, in less clear cases, testing might help the practitioner solidify the diagnosis.

When parents come to us, they've usually been through enough of the conventional process to have a diagnosis

1   T.H. Toh, V.W. Tan, P.S. Lau, A. Kiyu, "Accuracy of Modified Checklist for Autism in Toddlers M-CHAT) in Detecting Autism and Other Developmental Disorders in Community Clinics," *Journal of Autism and Developmental Disorders* 48, no. 1 (January 2018): 28–35.

of autism, but not much more. First and foremost, our job is to figure out if we agree with the diagnosis.

The range of autistic symptoms is huge, and many apparent symptoms can be a sign of something that is not exclusively autism. Recognizing the starting line means knowing where we aren't as well as where we are. Is it something genetic that cannot be treated? Are we dealing with a different disorder that looks like autism? Are there factors making the autistic symptoms worse, like seizures, sleep disorders, or infections?

To find out where a child stands, we begin with three basic steps. First, we recommend a genetic test called the chromosomal microarray, a powerful test for detecting certain genetic causes of developmental disabilities. We had one patient who received the diagnosis of autism but never had this foundational test completed. He came to see us when he was eleven years old and had been on the biomedical journey since he was three. All other providers made minimal improvement with him. After we recommended and he completed the CMA (chromosomal microarray), we found that this child had a major cluster of genes missing from his genome. These genes were also important for the formation of his eyes and kidneys. So this child, in fact, does not have autism. He has a rare genetic disorder that mimics symptoms of ASD. Instead of following up with neurology, this child really needed to be followed (or at least evaluated) by a geneticist, nephrologist, and ophthalmologist. Having different information on this child changed his trajectory of care.

Second, we need to understand if the child has a developmental delay or if they're having any type of seizures, because the incidence of seizures in patients with autism is very high. Third, we need to understand what type of delay the child has so we can choose the appropriate therapies to address it as early as possible. The earlier the intervention, the better the outcome for the child.

Basic genetic tests can rule out an array of genetic disorders in autism, but these only identify about 2 percent of cases. Even the initial Fragile X and chromosomal microarray tests don't reveal all abnormalities. More complete exome tests can go further, diving into significantly more genes to create a more complete genetic picture, but they still don't report on every gene that has a mutation in it. They're still not reporting on every single nucleotide polymorphism, or SNP, likely due to the fact that every human has lots of SNPs and mutations in their DNA. We recommend certain SNP testing (that has research behind it, primarily in the field of nutrigenomics) so that we can gain further insight into potential disruptions in nutritional, biochemical, and inflammatory pathways. These tests are a bit like transparent overlays we can place on the roadmap to add greater depth of details about the landscape we're dealing with.

It is common for children diagnosed with autism to have had an EEG done to rule out seizures. Unfortunately, this is likely just a routine sixty-minute EEG. This is a snapshot in time, and not as comprehensive as it could be. We often recommend extended studies (such as two or three days) where the child is monitored while awake and asleep. There are many companies that now provide this testing at home, so children no longer have to be admitted to the hospital to have a longer study done. Seizures are often very different from the grand mal epilepsy as portrayed in movies. They can also take the shape of weird repetitive behaviors or aggressive outbursts or even a staring spell that makes it impossible to get the child's attention. Some people may not even realize it is happening. We saw a teenage girl with autism who was having severe behavioral issues with aggression and perseveration. After we conducted a forty-eight-hour EEG study, it revealed she was having seizures while she was asleep. This new information helped us guide our treatment and medications in a new direction, and she reached a place of stabilization that previously seemed impossible to reach. As noted above, approximately 22 percent of patients with autism end up having epilepsy,[2] so our

---

2   Patrick F. Bolton, "Epilepsy in Autism: Features and Correlates," *British Journal of Psychiatry* 198, no. 4 (April 2011): 289–294.

time spent investigating seizures with longer studies has proven well worth the extra effort.

KEEP GOING

Painting a complete picture of a child's autism requires a lot of forward momentum. Many parents need encouragement to keep going, especially if they haven't seen significant improvement in their child yet. We do see some level of improvement in most of the children that we treat, but getting there might depend on trying a few different approaches.

When we first opened our practice, for example, we saw one family with two girls on the spectrum. We did a lot of testing and supplementation with them, and we saw improvements here and there, mostly with dietary changes. Sadly, the parents were not able to maintain a consistently clean diet, and we did not see them for a while. Recently, those same parents read an article on our Facebook page about PANDAS (pediatric autoimmune neuropsychiatric syndrome) and the mom came back in. The article resonated with her because her child showed many of the symptoms associated with the condition. We investigated it, and sure enough, she had PANDAS. We targeted her immune system, and she has since improved greatly.

We can't emphasize enough how important it is to keep

looking, because everyone will uncover different layers. Sometimes we hit on a shortcut; for example, if we start in the gut for one patient, balance out their bowel movements, and the patient shows great improvement in talking, anxiety, stimming, and eye contact, there might not be a need to keep testing. Every roadmap is different.

For more complex cases, testing can give more concrete personalized data that helps us prescribe a precise plan of care. We implement the plan, give it time to work, and then reevaluate to determine the next step. Sometimes, the next step is to keep doing the same thing for months. Other times, we jump right into organic acids testing because sleep is poor, or we do neurotransmitter testing because anxiety is an issue. When we see patients, we are going to use our best scientific judgment to prioritize what's important for treating a child, but it takes time. It's important not to give up if something doesn't work the first time.

Honestly, the process can take just three months, or it could take three years. This is not conventional one-ill-one-pill type medicine. We understand that it can get tiring to do seven or eight things at once over a long period of time, but consistency is extremely important to outcomes. In fact, the patients who see the most improved outcomes are the ones that follow our treatment protocols to the letter. They are diligent and consistent. We are always willing to work with parents to make the process as smooth and fluid as possible, but their commitment to the process and plan is critical to its success.

ASSESS THE PROGRESS

How long a family keeps going with treatments is a tough question, because there are so many variables, starting with the individual's situation and the treatments themselves. Some people can keep at it for a long time because they have the resources—insurance reimburses for the treatment—while some people stop because they just can't afford to pay for an array of different tests.

Unfortunately, insurances deem a lot of specialized testing "experimental" and are unwilling to cover the testing, leaving the parents responsible for the out-of-pocket costs. We find this heartbreaking, because the specialized/functional laboratories that support our clinical data are just as rigorously certified (and often more valid and reliable) than the lab companies insurance has deemed "in network" and therefore covered.

Changes can seem incremental, which is why it's so useful to document the baseline for each patient. We encourage family members to take videos and pictures of the child so they can look back and see how far the child has come. We also offer benchmarks so parents can see how their child improves over time. Another way we track results is through MSQ scoring, a multiple symptom questionnaire utilized by the Institute of Functional Medicine, which everyone fills out on their initial visit. It helps track problems in the mind, emotions, gut, skin, and more, so we recognize improvements in different areas. This helps parents acknowledge what has improved over time.

The landscape shifts over time too. Patients may move from frequent visits to yearly, but we try to follow up with patients because there is always something new to offer that might help improve their lives. Our knowledge and technology are always changing.

RECOGNIZE THE ROADBLOCKS

Sometimes, we find what we're looking for, but then we hit a roadblock. We discover there's little we can do about it. There are rare cases in which we discover genetic variants that are impossible to change. If a patient has Fragile X, triple X, or trisomy 21, for example, we won't be able to change the structure of the chromosome, but that doesn't mean the end of the road for treatment. We can still help that child optimize their total health so that they can have the best chance to maximize their own potential.

We know some Down syndrome patients who have been told there's no help available. We disagree. Some low-functioning Down syndrome babies become more high-functioning when we optimize other aspects of their physiology. We can still look into their methylation and optimize nutrient deficiencies, for example (topics we'll cover in detail later in this book). One of our patients with Down syndrome was struggling with aggression and severe behavior issues. His parents and siblings felt that they could not have a relationship with him because they were afraid of him. After working to heal his gut, changing his diet, and addressing underlying infections, he is a different child. His mom reports that they have their child back, and he now plays with his siblings!

Parents should keep in mind that the limits we face today are fast giving way to new treatments. For instance, we are only at the frontier of understanding what is in the DNA of our microbiome that can help alter the expression of our own DNA. While someone might be stuck now, it doesn't mean that will be the case in the future. Medical science is changing at a formidable pace. There were over 285,000 medical citations published in the US in 2017 alone. That does not include anything published internationally, which is often where we glean groundbreaking medical content.[3]

---

3   "MEDLINE Citation Counts by Year of Publication (as of mid-December 2017)" *PubMed*, https://www.nlm.nih.gov/bsd/medline_cit_counts_yr_pub.html.

SET DESTINATION GOALS

When parents have gathered as much information about their starting point as they can, it's time to set some goals for the trip. Every family has different goals. For example, parents of a nonverbal child are often desperate to have their child speak. They are focused entirely on doing anything to help the child express themselves verbally. Parents of children with higher-functioning autism, though, might pursue goals about social interaction and connectedness. Some patients reach such a high level of functioning that we don't even know if they would classify as being on the spectrum anymore. We have one such patient who is very intelligent, is doing well in school, and has become social, but he tends to withdraw so he can hand flap in private to soothe himself. For him, decreasing his anxiety (which increases his need to hand flap) and giving him additional coping tools that don't prompt him to withdraw have been our primary goals.

Obtaining the goal can be easy for some patients and more challenging for others. One of our patients, a twenty-four-year-old man with Asperger's, was so rigid with his schedule it got in the way of treating his gut issues. We did some blood work and stool study and found he had a dysbiotic, or harmful gut bacteria, called H. pylori. When Emily went over his labs with him, he revealed he had previously seen a gastroenterologist who treated this; however, his treatment failed. Again, when we tried to get him on medications, he couldn't keep up with them due to his need for rigid scheduling. For example, he wouldn't take a certain medication that needed to be taken with food because he didn't eat breakfast on certain days (due to work obligations) and felt he couldn't change his schedule. Once we were able to map out a very detailed and simple handwritten plan for him, with clear times and schedule modifications, he became compliant to our treatment, and the H. pylori was eventually eradicated. His gut needed medical intervention, but so did his rigidity. Addressing both pieces was the breakthrough he needed to receive the care he required.

Some families hope to decrease aggression. It's a huge challenge in autism, with a variety of causes. A child can have a genetic predisposition, such as a monoamine A gene that doesn't help them degrade, or break down, serotonin. Another child might become aggressive before seizures. For him, that means we need to get the seizures under control. For yet another child, the aggression might be severe—stabbing other children with pencils in the classroom, for example. Aggression can be linked to an imbalance of glutamate in the brain. There are medications and supplements that can help mitigate glutamate excess. We have both seen that targeting this imbalance can have profound effects on the agitation, irritability, aggression, and anxiety.[4] It's heartbreaking to talk to parents who worry that their child might seriously hurt someone else. In so many cases, the main goal is safety. We want to try to do everything in our power to help people come closer to essential and necessary goals like these.

Because treatments can have their challenges, we work to keep families motivated. Sometimes it's easier for parents to continue working toward a goal if they understand the data behind it, so we might meet with parents and show them the relevant studies. Sometimes we go over test results as we go along to show them concrete evidence to support how we are trying to help their child. Our work with our patients is scientifically driven, specific to the child, and is a partnership between parent and provider to ultimately restore balance where the child needs it.

For people who don't have the resources to fund regular testing, we can also use our past experience to help them. We know what has worked for a majority of autistic children with similar symptoms in the past. We have the information parents need to map their journey forward, but they have to be willing to try something new, follow through and be consistent with treatments, and follow up as requested. Goals are dynamic and changing for every

---

4   Afaf El-Ansary and Laila Al-Ayadhi, "GABAergic/glutamergic Imbalance Relative to Exessive Neuroinflammation in Autism Spectrum Disorders," *Journal of Neuroinflammation* 11 (2014): 189.

child, but with determination, we may arrive at a destination they never thought we could achieve.

CHAPTER THREE

—

FUELING UP FOR THE JOURNEY

Once parents establish a location and set their initial goals for their child, nutrition is the most common place to start. Food is important. That may seem obvious, but it often gets overlooked. Food is fuel for our bodies. If we put regular gas in a car that ran on diesel, it wouldn't run.

In a similar way, food impacts how a child develops and how cells detox, recover, and rebuild.

Some families come to us from other practitioners who told them diet wouldn't make a difference for their child. Our response, only half-joking, is to ask, "Well, what would happen if you decided not to eat for thirty days? What would happen if you just ate candy?" Of course, food makes a difference. Any child would be near death without food. We can all agree it does something to our bodies. Many parents have witnessed their children getting hyper after eating lots of sugar or artificially dyed food. When they see that, they realize the effects food can have on a child.

To begin, let's look at the real reason nutrition is so important in treating autism. It has a profound effect on inflammation in the body.

NUTRITION AND INFLAMMATION

Food helps determine if a body goes in an inflammatory or anti-inflammatory direction. The most basic definition of inflammation is that it is a response to tissue injury or infection, in which we see pain, heat, redness, and swelling. When we eat food or ingest a substance that our body doesn't like, we experience inflammation that we may not see on the outside of our body.

When the body is burdened by inflammation, it becomes so dysregulated that it starts to see even healthy things as foreign invaders that need to be repelled. The body begins to attack itself.[1]

In autism, the body may be under attack on many different levels because the person is eating inflammatory foods, inhaling inflammatory substances, or ingesting inflammatory chemicals. This exposure creates an upregulation of the immune system, making the body work very hard to achieve homeostasis, or balance.

The body is always trying to achieve homeostasis, or balance. When we wake up and our body signals us to drink water because we're dehydrated after eight or nine hours without fluids, it's trying to regain homeostasis. But if a person wakes up and drinks water with fluoride and heavy metals in it, eats a bowl of wheat-based cereal with food dyes and milk, and then puts on perfume and lotion, they have given their body a lot to process. An inflammatory response is likely.

When that inflammation happens day to day, minute to minute, the body can develop a chaotic response and start to develop symptoms of chronic disease. In the case of

---

1   N.R. Klatt, L.D. Harris, et al., "Compromised Gastrointestinal Integrity in Pigtail Macaques is Associated with Increased Microbial Translocation, Immune Activation, and IL-17 Production in the Absence of SIV Infection," *Mucosal Immunology* (July 2010): 387–398.

a sprained ankle, it's easy to spot the inflammation—the ankle is red and swollen and can't withstand pressure—but in the case of chronic disease, it's often more covert.

Chronic illness arises from the invisible but constant strain of inflammation on the body. In autism, the comorbid conditions we see over and over again are immune dysregulation, chronic infections, chronic inflammatory gut disease, chronic irritable bowels, skin issues, headaches, and seizures, all of which can be caused by autoimmune responses triggered by inflammation.[2]

ANTI-INFLAMMATORY FOODS

The good news is that what we eat can change the level of inflammation in the body. Any food we put in our bodies has the potential to increase or decrease inflammation. Because inflammation can amplify the negative symptoms and behaviors of autism—and even trigger autism itself—our goal is to decrease inflammation by giving the body the right kind of fuel.

There are many anti-inflammatory foods, but choosing the right options depends on an individual's immune system. What causes inflammation in one patient may

---

2   Martha R. Herbert and Matthew P, Anderson, "An Expanding Spectrum of Autism Models: From Fixed Developmental Defects to Reversible Functional Impairments," in *Autism*, ed. A.W. Zimmerman (Totowa, NJ: Human Press, 2008): 429-463.

be a nutritional powerhouse for another. Some people are allergic to beets, for instance, but for others, they are an incredible source of antioxidants and phytonutrients.

It's therefore not surprising that there's not one universal diet that works for every child with autism. Some need a low histamine diet, some need a low-phenol or low-salicylate diet, and others need to go gluten- or dairy-free.

That said, we can make some generalizations. In general, fruits and vegetables are anti-inflammatory. Particularly valuable are cruciferous vegetables high in sulforaphanes, like broccoli, cauliflower, and kale. Low glycemic fruits like berries and apples tend to be anti-inflammatory options, too. (Note, fruit can be over-consumed, too; ingesting two servings of sugar at every meal can be proinflammatory.)[3]

Most people should also include foods high in alpha-linolenic acid, which are precursors to omega-3 fatty acids. Omega-3 fatty acids can potentially modulate both neuroinflammatory components and gut imbalances in autism.[4] The Western diet tends to be unbalanced, favoring omega-6 over omega-3. Having too much omega-6

---

3   M Bahniwal, J.P. Little, A. Klegeris, "High Glucose Enhances Neurotoxicity and Inflammatory Cytokine Secretion by Stimulated Human Astrocytes," *Current Alzheimer Research* 14, no.7 (2017): 731–41.

4   Charlotte Madore et al., "Neuroinflammation in Autism: Plausible Role of Maternal Inflammation, Dietary Omega 3, and Microbiota," *Neural Plasticity* (2016).

can lead to high levels of arachidonic acid, which is an extremely inflammatory substance for our bodies. An omega-fatty-acid profile can reveal an imbalance, which can be treated with omega-3-rich foods like chia seeds, hemp seeds, walnuts, and even wild game. Vegetarians who don't want to put animal products into their bodies can get omega-3 fatty acids from algae, chia, walnuts, and flax oil. These have linoleic acid which becomes EPA and DHA, the most important elements in omega-3s.[5]

Many people choose to supplement with fish oil, but they may not be getting an optimal dose. Less than 1,500 milligrams provides little to no anti-inflammatory effect, while anything over 7,000 milligrams offers no additional benefit. A small child might take 1,500 milligrams, and older children might need 5,000 milligrams. For autism, it has been shown that a higher EPA to DHA ratio can prove beneficial for speech and cognitive function.[6] The source of the fish oil is also something to be mindful of since larger fish tend to have higher levels of

5   D. Mozaffarian et al., "Dietary Intake of Trans Fatty Acids and Systemic Inflammation in Women," *The American Journal of Clinical Nutrition* 79, Issue 4 (April 1, 2004): 606–12; D. Mozaffarian et al., Trans Fatty Acids and Systemic Inflammation in Heart Failure," American Journal of Clinical Nutrition 80, no. 6 (Dec. 2004): 1521–25.

6   F.P. Amminger et al., "Omega-3 Fatty Acids Supplementation in Children with Autism: A Double-blind Randomized, Placebo-controlled Pilot Study," *Biological Psychiatry* 61, no. 4 (February 2007): 551–3; S Bent, et al., "A Pilot Randomized Controlled Trial of Omega-3 Fatty Acids for Autism Spectrum Disorder," *Journal of Autism and Developmental Disorders* 41, no. 5 (May 2011): 545–54; Y.O. Ooi et al., "Omega-3 Fatty Acids in the Management of Autism Spectrum Disorders: Findings from an Open-Label Pilot Study in Singapore," *European Journal of Clinical Nutrition* 69, no. 8 (August 2015): 969–71.

mercury. Readers looking for a place to start can check out our list of great omega-3s on our website (http://store-neuronutritionassociates-com.mybigcommerce.com/) under essential fatty acids.

OTHER NUTRITION BASICS: EAT FATS, NOT SUGAR

In addition to looking at anti-inflammatory diet options for our patients, we try to ensure enough of the right kind of fat for brain growth. That means avoiding things like partially hydrogenated oils or vegetable oils and focusing on other oils like nut, algae, olive, and avocado oils.[7] The right fats are really good for us and high in alpha-linolenic acid.

These good fats are essential for children's brain growth because the brain keeps growing into the twenties. We always tell our teenage patients, "You might think you know more than your parents, but their brains are actually bigger because your brain isn't done growing." Oils like coconut and avocado can be used in high temperature cooking and are wonderful for brain fuel. The medium chain triglycerides found in coconut oil are thought to be a super fuel for your brain. We support cooking with olive oil as well, just at lower temperatures (less than 300 degrees Fahrenheit) so the oil stays stable and does not

---

7   C. Julia et al., "Dietary Patterns and Risk of Elevated C-reactive Protein Concentrations 12 Years Later," *British Journal of Nutrition* 110, no. 4 (August 2013): 747–54.

go rancid. People worry about eating too much fat, but if we're eating healthy fats, that's not really possible. Fat itself is essential, especially for children with neurodevelopmental disorders such as autism.[8] Half of the brain's dry weight is just fat. Having a healthier level of fat has even been shown to reduce psychosis and chances of suicide in children.[9] Fat lines every single cell in our body, helping with transmission of signals in and out of the cell. It's not fat that makes us overweight; it's sugar.

Sugar is the real culprit.[10] Not only is it the main factor in weight gain, sugar even changes healthy oils and fats into unhealthy oils and fats. Sugar upregulates an enzyme called delta-5 desaturase, which takes good omega-3 fatty acids we get from things like chia, hemp, and walnuts, and shunts them into arachidonic acid, the most proinflammatory fat possible.

Many parents don't think their children are consuming much sugar, but there are often hidden sources. Maybe they don't eat candy bars, but they love French toast for

8   A.J. Richardson and P. Montgomery, "The Oxford-Durham Study: A Randomized, Controlled Trial of Dietary Supplementation with Fatty Acids in Children with Developmental Coordination Disorder." *Pediatrics* 115, no. 5 (May 2005): 1360–66.

9   G. Paul Amminger et al., "Longer-term Outcome in the Prevention of Psychotic Disorders by the Vienna Omega-3 Study," *Nature Communications* (August 11, 2015); and MD Lewis et al., "Suicide Deaths of Active-Duty US Military and Omega-3 Fatty-Acid Status: A Case-Control Comparison," *Journal of Clinical Psychiatry* 72, no. 12 (December 2011): 1585–90.

10   M Bahniwal, J.P. Little, A. Klegeris, "High Glucose Enhances Neurotoxicity and Inflammatory Cytokine Secretion by Stimulated Human Astrocytes," *Current Alzheimer Research* 14, no.7 (2017): 731–41.

breakfast and a sandwich for lunch. We had one patient come in whose parent said had an excellent diet. We did his labs and found he was diabetic. He had high insulin, high hemoglobin A1c, and a fatty liver, which primarily comes from sugar turning into fat and "clogging" up the liver. We had to curb his carbohydrate intake to no more than two servings of grains a day and no more than twenty added grams of sugar. The parents had to start reading labels. When people start reading labels, they often find it alarming to see how much sugar and high fructose corn syrup is in everything, even a jar of dill pickles.

It's not always easy to reduce sugars because they're addictive. Rats given bottles of cocaine water and sugar water will quickly choose the sugar.[11] For those rats, sugar was more addictive than cocaine. We often recommend reducing refined sugar intake and using natural sweeteners like honey and maple syrup instead, but in very small amounts. Stay away from artificial sweeteners except for stevia (raw and organic). Some people sweeten using dates, coconut sugar, and bananas. Bananas even have the added benefit of being a great sweetener for baking since they can substitute for eggs and are high in prebiotic fiber.

The thing is, a lot of patients with autism love carbs. They'll eat breads and drink sugary drinks all day long.

---

11   H.B. Madsen and S.H. Ahmed, "Drug Versus Sweet Reward: Greater Attraction to and
      Preference for Sweet Versus Drug Cues," *Addiction Biology* 20, no. 3 (May 2015): 433–44.

Their parents often have trouble getting them to eat anything else. That makes it hard to get healthy fats into their diet. One method we recommend is to add a smoothie a day to the menu, made with things like coconut oil, avocados, and healthy omegas like flax and chia. Smoothies also offer a way of adding fruits, vegetables, and even supplements into the diet. Basically, it's a fun way to disguise foods that the child may be avoiding.

Not all children get on board the smoothie train easily, though, and many people come in thinking there's no way their child is going to eat anything healthy. We've found that's a self-fulfilling prophecy. It is possible to turn around a child's dietary habits. It just takes a bit of work. Parents may have to try a little tough love. We know it's hard to see a child refuse to eat, but letting them have soda or just drink milk all day isn't going to help them. Parents should start small. Some parents replace one item on a child's plate at a time so as not to shock the child. Then, week-by-week, they replace more items until the diet is noticeably different. In our years of treating patients, we have only seen a child refuse to eat as long as a day and half. When they are hungry, they will eat, even if it is something they typically won't touch. With patience, parents can turn their picky child around. We remind them they are not responsible for what their child eats, but they are responsible for what they provide their child to eat.

FUEL THE BRAIN

Fruits, vegetables, meats, and proteins offer more than energy. They provide micro- and macronutrients that create cofactors for psychological processes that are incredibly important to mood, learning, behavior, and development.

For instance, neurotransmitters aren't produced by organs on their own. We have to create them through a methylation and biochemical process. This process is dependent on many cofactors of nutrition like B12, B6, methyl folate, and zinc. If we aren't giving our bodies cofactors, it's like baking a cake and omitting a cup of flour. The product is not going to be good if it's missing ingredients. Our body's recipe calls for a phytonutrient rich diet full of fruits, vegetables, proteins, and fats.[12] It's hard to expect children to eat vegetables and healthy foods when they are offered hot dogs, mac and cheese, and pizza at most meals.

Skip the kid's menu. Children's menus at restaurants usually feature all beige foods and no vegetables. It's aggravating, because children are the ones who need those nutrients the most. Eating off the kid's menu is like putting water in the gas tank of a car. Sure, the tank is full, but the car is not going to go anywhere.

---

12   A.L. Miller, "The Methylation, Neurotransmitter, and Antioxidant Connections Between Folate and Depression," *Alternative Medicine Review* 13, no. 3 (Sep. 2008): 216–26.

For adults, the aha moment often comes when they witness the effects of removing gluten, casein, or grains from their child's diet. Foods like dairy can actually produce an opioid type effect in the brain, causing a morphine-like chemical that mimics addiction.[13] Autistic children have realized gains when eliminating these foods from their diet, even a reduction in seizures.[14] One parent told us she saw her child "come out of a fog" when she removed dairy. This child was now paying attention and looking at her.

The reason diet changes can help the brain is that the brain and the gut are connected via the vagus nerve. When the gut is inflamed, the brain's inflammatory balance is also affected. Clearing out stomach inflammation can have a neurological benefit, as well as an overall body benefit. We often see eczema clear up because we stop a parent from accidentally feeding their child foods that they are allergic to. The results can be very powerful.

FEED THE MITOCHONDRIA

One promising use for nutrition in autism is to treat mitochondrial dysfunction. A lot of people come to us

---

13   O. Sokolov et al., "Autistic Children Display Elevated Urine Levels of Bovine Casomorphin-7 Immunoreactivity." *Peptides* 56 (June 2014): 68–71.

14   M.R. Herbert and J.A. Buckley, "Autism and Dietary Therapy: Case Report and Review of the Literature," *Journal of Child Neurology* 28, no. 8 (August 2013): 975–82.

wanting to know if their child has this disorder. We'll cover mitochondria extensively in the chapter devoted to the immune system, but for now, we'll just note mitochondria need a lot of key nutrients to function properly. Nutrition is so important to mitochondria that the IFM put together a "Mito Diet"[15] which is an anti-inflammatory, low-glycemic, gluten-free, low-grain, high-quality-fat diet designed to boost mitochondrial health.

FIND THE RIGHT FUEL

All of the information we've shared in this chapter is useful and can be empowering for families because they now have some things to try at home. But many families look at the list of options (reproduced here) and feel overwhelmed. GAPS diet, low FODMAPs, ketogenic, Feingold...where do they start?

---

15   Institute for Functional Medicine, https://www.ifm.org/

NAME OF DIET	RECOMMENDATION FOR DIET	SPECIFICS
Gluten/casein/ soy free	Recommended to start for all autistic patients. Research by Dr. Harumi Jyonouchi shows that 91 percent of people with ASD who were put on a strict GFCFSF diet improved. Most recent studies done that show no improvement were only done for several weeks and the studies were "designed to fail."	No gluten (wheat, rye, barley, spelt, kamut, most oats). No casein (animal milk products).
Low Fodmap	Can be helpful for GI symptoms such as bloating, gas, burping, stomach pain, intolerance of carbohydrates or complex sugars. Very successful treatment for IBS.	No fermentable carbohydrates for introductory phase. No oligosaccharides, disaccharides, monosaccharides, or polyols.
SCD	Can be helpful for fructose malabsorption, intolerance of carbohydrates, and symptoms such as gas, bloating, burping.	No lactose, sucrose, maltose, isomaltose. No grains (corn, rice, starches, certain beans) or sugar, except honey. No polysaccharides.
Low histamine	Recommended if child has ++ DaO enzyme or intolerance with high histamine foods.	Avoid meals with multiple high histamine foods, or take enzymes with meals. Some foods include processed meats, avocados, dairy, banana, spinach, tomatoes, and alcohol.
Low phenols	Phenols include salicylates, amines, and glutamate foods. Recommended for children who have hyperactivity, aggression, inappropriate laughter, or skin rashes twenty minutes after eating a food high in phenols.	Avoid food dyes, tomatoes, apples, peanuts, bananas, red grapes, vanilla, artificial flavors.

NAME OF DIET	RECOMMENDATION FOR DIET	SPECIFICS
Autoimmune Paleo (AIP)	Recommended for those with autoimmune disorders—cuts out grains and all inflammatory foods.	Introductory phase includes consuming bone broth for two to three days to allow gut to heal, then introducing certain vegetables and meats.
Ketogenic	Very low carb, high fat, and moderate protein. Helpful for those with epilepsy or seizure disorders. Also recommended for other neurological concerns.	Focus on foods high in fat (cheese, avocados, eggs, coconut oil, olive oil, low carb veggies, seafood, yogurt).
Feingold	Helpful diet for hyperactivity and poor behaviors that eliminates certain additives, colors, and chemicals from foods.	Avoid artificial preservatives, flavors, and synthetic food colorings: MSG, sodium benzoate, nitrites, sulfites, and BHA.
GAPS	Similar to SCD diet; helps treat chronic inflammation related to damage of the gut lining. Has several stages that start with bone broth and increase introduction of different foods.	Avoid sugar, molasses, maple syrup, corn syrup, aspartame, sweets, alcohol, canned and processed foods, grains (rice, corn, rye, oats, wheat), starchy veggies, milk, beans, coffee, and soy.
Body Ecology	Helpful for systemic candida and imbalanced flora in the gut.	Avoid all sugars including fruit. Only sour fruit is allowed in the beginning (lemons, limes, black currants, and cranberries). Then you can add grapefruit, kiwi, and green apples. Add in fermented foods eventually (coconut kefir, raw sauerkraut, and cultured veggies).

How we shape someone's diet depends on their situation and symptoms. For example, if a patient is gassy, constantly burping, with a distended belly, we will likely recommend a Specific Carbohydrate Diet or low FODMAP diet. Sometimes we prescribe a diet immediately, while other times, we do tests first.

Often, the best place to start is with an elimination diet because removing potentially troublesome foods from the diet and reintroducing them one-by-one will provide the most accurate information about how the body is handling these foods. The basic protocol involves removing potentially inflammatory food groups from the diet for a minimum of twenty-one days because that is how long the immunoglobulin response to those foods takes to decrease the burden by at least half. Just a few days is not enough time to see how the immune system will respond. After at least twenty-one days, each food is reintroduced, and the patient's symptoms are monitored. When reintroducing foods, we do it one item at a time, for two servings a day, for at least three days in a row. The protocol requires at least three consecutive days because we need to give the body adequate time to show its tolerance, because there can be a delayed reaction in the body. If the patient's symptoms come back, they might have a problem with this food. Common foods to work with on allergies and sensitivities are gluten-containing grains, dairy products, sugar, soy products, shellfish, peanuts, eggs, beef, and pork.

As with all treatments, dietary approaches need to be tailored to the individual, and we need to look closely at what's going on. A lot of our work here is like detective work. We have to follow the clues to the source to solve the case.

PARENTS HAVE THE POWER

We recognize that dietary changes can seem daunting. We understand how difficult it is to have a child reject new and unusual foods. Parents want them to eat *something*, so a PB&J sandwich seems good enough. Still, we believe parents have the power to shape their child's nutrition. There are strategies that can help them make the change. For instance, they can slowly phase out certain foods, or make substitute versions from scratch. Homemade "Paleo nuggets" go a long way in many families. Parents can hide the vegetables in smoothies, or work with the child's texture issues by offering baby food pouches with veggies. Appendix A at the end of the book offers some basic recipes to get started.

Parents should feel free to get creative because there's never a good enough reason to ignore nutrition. Like everything else in this book, we encourage parents to keep digging. That might mean going further than straight diet adjustments. It might mean genetic testing to determine if the child isn't breaking down histamines or processing B12 efficiently or lacks certain enzymes. Research has shown that dietary and supplemental intervention can help children on the spectrum improve developmentally. While changing your child's diet might seem like an impossible task, it likely will be well worth it.[16]

No matter how tempting it is to just pull off the road, we urge parents to keep going because, chances are, they can find options that will improve their child's health and life in significant ways.

---

16 James B. Adams et al., "Comprehensive Nutritional and Dietary Intervention for Autism Spectrum Disorder—A Randomized, Controlled 12-Month Trial," *Nutrients* 10, no. 3 (March 2018): 369.

CHAPTER FOUR

GET ON THE GUT HIGHWAY

To parents who feel overwhelmed on this journey and don't know where to start, we say, "Find the gut highway and jump on." Nutrition is incredibly important, but the best nutrition in the world won't help if a person is not able to digest, absorb, and assimilate food into energy signals for the body. That's why functional medicine starts with gut health.

The gut, also called the enteric nervous system, stretches from the mouth to the anus. It contains 70 percent of our immune system. It's where we make the majority of our neurotransmitters and where food is converted to signals that drive our physiological processes.[1] In short, the gut disseminates information throughout the body. Anything we put in our gut will be shared with the rest of the body, which is why disturbances in digestion, absorption, and assimilation—frequently triggered by inflammation—can lead to chronic disease.

Autism and gut problems are commonly known to go together. They're also called comorbidities, as previously mentioned. Usually, the gut is already in a state of chaos when people come in. Patients often have accidents called encopresis, or chronic constipation, for example, where they are stooling small amounts into their underwear and sometimes are unaware that this is happening. It's also common for families to come to us with a child who is having diarrhea four times a day. They're often surprised to hear that the issue may have as much to do with the balance of bacteria in the gut as it does with their child's diet. The gut's environment can be affected by many things—parasites, intestinal inflammation, bacteria from mom, antibiotics, and steroids, for example—that most people don't think about. It's important that we do,

---

1   Qinrui Li, Ying Han, Angel Belle C. and Randi J. Hagerman, "The Gut Microbiota and Autism Spectrum Disorders," *Frontiers in Cellular Neuroscience* 11, no. 120 (2017): 120.

because if a child doesn't have a balanced gut, it's hard to heal the whole body. For example, a patient with a leaky gut that hasn't healed might not fully benefit from a diet that would otherwise be healing.

We also consider other factors, like what they are eating, their lifestyle, and their stress levels. Surprisingly, stress can influence the microbiome even more than diet.[2] It shifts the flora in a negative way, which can manipulate neurotransmitters, affecting serotonin and dopamine levels. A lot of the feelings we feel, like the butterflies of anxiety, is just communication between the gut and the brain. Because the gut communicates so heavily with the brain, we look for gut issues when a patient is not sleeping well or seems depressed or anxious.

It's important to evaluate stress levels in our patients too; ironically, treatments can be overstimulating. Children may experience an overload of noises, activities, therapists, colors, and other environmental input throughout their day. We have one autistic patient who is only four years old and is in ABA therapy forty hours a week. She's not getting her daily nap and is overly tired when she gets home. We encourage parents to try to maintain a normal

---

2   Michael T. Bailey and Christopher L. Coe, "Maternal Separation Disrupts the Integrity of the Intestinal Microflora in Infant Rhesus Monkeys," *Developmental Psychobiology* (August 24, 1999); Jane A. Foster, Linda Rinamin and John F. Cryan, "Stress and the Gut-Brain Axis: Regulation by the Microbiome," *Neurobiology of Stress 7* (December 2017): 124-36.

schedule for these children and incorporate activities to lower stress levels.

HIT THE MICROBIOME MOTORWAY

With most patients, we start investigating the gut by asking about bowel patterns and reviewing the Bristol stool chart, a medically validated tool that shows how different formations of stool can give clues as to what is going on in the gut (such as inflammation or enzymatic dysfunction). It's essentially a diagram of poop and what it looks like. Is it hard? Soft? A little in the middle? What's the shape? Parents can usually help with identification, as silly as this may seem.

Using a chart helps us get specific. Is the child having diarrhea multiple times a day, or have they been constipated since they were born?

BRISTOL STOOL CHART		
Type 1	Separate hard lumps	SEVERE CONSTIPATION
Type 2	Lumpy and sausage like	MILD CONSTIPATION
Type 3	A sausage shape with cracks in the surface	NORMAL
Type 4	Like a smooth, soft sausage or snake	NORMAL
Type 5	Soft blobs with clear-cut edges	LACKING FIBRE
Type 6	Mushy consistency with ragged edges	MILD DIARRHEA
Type 7	Liquid consistency with no solid pieces	SEVERE DIARRHEA

A good way to investigate the gut is looking at stool, so we often will request the family collect a stool sample. Yes, we know that collecting your child's stool is not the most exciting thing, but it can provide so much information! A majority of the children we see are missing major species of bacteria in their guts because they missed some foundational opportunities for establishing their microbiome. The first year of life is incredibly important for giving a child that firm foundation of flora. Many of these children were born by C-section, so they missed out on a critical period of colonization through the vaginal canal during birth. Many were not breastfed, which is another opportunity to share beneficial bacteria which helps establish the microbiome in those early months of life. They may have also taken multiple rounds of antibiotics within the first year of life, wiping out certain colonies of beneficial bacteria. Many autistic children, even when they're eating solid foods, have a limited diet. Microbial diversity depends a lot on the food we eat.[3]

After we establish the basics, we explain the jobs of the gut and its connection to the immune system and brain. We emphasize microbiome health, which is the accumulation of bacterial cells in the gastrointestinal tract. Many people are surprised to find these bacterial cells

3   H. Bisgaard et al., "Reduced Diversity of the Intestinal Microbiota during Infancy Is Associated with Increased Risk of Allergic Disease at School Age," *Journal of Allergy and Clinical Immunology* 128, no. 3 (September 2011): 646–652.

outnumber the host cells ten to one.[4] Their genes outnumber the host's by an estimated one hundred to one![5] There are trillions and trillions of bacteria in our gut that help us regulate health and autoimmunity. They are from two major categories: bacteroides and firmicutes. The balance of these two colonies of bacteria is incredibly important.

The truth is that as much as 90 percent of people don't have a balanced microbiome. In a world where fast food is the norm, people don't eat well, they work high-stress jobs, and don't sleep well, it's hard to get that microbiome back in balance. Most of us don't even manage to achieve a fifty-fifty balance of good to bad bacteria, when a more ideal ratio is eighty-five to fifteen. Not surprisingly, most children have an unbalanced microbiome.

NEW OPTIONS IN MICROBIOME BALANCING

It's an exciting time in microbiome research, though. We believe we're on the brink of understanding what each species of bacteria does for the gut. Just as we've long known different types of pathogenic bacteria cause illness, we now know that beneficial bacteria can promote

---

4   Ron Sender, Shai Fuchs and Ron Milo, "Revised Estimates for the Number of Human and Bacteria Cells in the Body," *PLoS Biology* 14, no. 8 (August 19, 2016).

5   Lawrence A. David et al., "Diet Rapidly and Reproducibly Alters the Human Gut Microbiome," *Nature* 505 (January 23, 2014): 559–63.

wellness. For example, lactobacillus rhamnosus is one species that studies show decreases diarrhea in children when they get infected with rotavirus.[6] Bifidobacterium has been reported to be effective for helping with constipation. There are also strains of strep salivarius we now know can decrease the adherence of strep pyogenes, a strain of strep that causes acute illness, which makes people susceptible to strep throat.[7]

In the wake of these exciting findings, companies are emerging that make claims they can "map your microbiome." Parents should realize that they are not all equally reliable, though they can be useful. Many, like uBiome, show bacterial markers; others, like Viome, can even recommend what foods to add to or remove from the diet. These are consumer market tests, and anyone can order them, without a doctor's order.

We find doing stool testing through rigorous and CLIA-certified functional medicine labs such as Doctor's Data and Diagnostic Solutions gives us the most information so we can really work to balance the microbiome. Some of this testing is available on our practice website, even

---

6   N. Pant et al., "Effective Prophylaxis Against Rotavirus Diarrhea Using a Combination of
      Lactobacillus rhamnosus GG and Antibodies," *BMC Microbiology* 7 (September 27, 2007): 7-86.

7   F. Di Pierro et al., "Use of *Streptococcus salivarius* K12 in the Prevention of Streptococcal and
      Viral Pharyngotonsillitis in Children," *Drug, Healthcare and Patient Safety* 6 (February 13,
      2014): 15-20.

for folks who are not established patients: NeuronutritionAssociates.com.

Another new and promising treatment gaining popularity in the autism world is the fecal transplant. A fecal transplant involves taking fecal matter from a healthy donor and introducing it into a sick person's microbiome. More parents are choosing to try this with their autistic children. The procedure is FDA approved to eradicate a pathogen known as C. difficile (a bacteria that grows when there is an overuse of antibiotics and causes virulent diarrhea) and often there is remission of symptoms within twenty-four hours.[8] It has promise, but there are risks. Parents have to be careful about the source of the stool, because although the donor may live a healthy lifestyle, they may have become tolerant to some pathogens that could be dangerous to the donor recipient. We see the potential for this procedure, but we aren't completely on board with parents attempting this on their own until there is a more controlled and regulated way to do it.

PRACTICAL SOLUTIONS FOR GUT ISSUES

Outside of complex genetic testing and cutting-edge procedures, there are many ways parents can optimize gut functioning in their children. We've found many patients

---

8   Dae-Wook Kang et al., "Microbiota Transfer Therapy Alters Gut Ecosystem and Improves Gastrointestinal and Autism Symptoms: An Open-Label Study," *Microbiome* 5, no. 10 (2017).

improve when they are able to reduce exposure to harmful inputs like environmental toxins and increase helpful inputs like probiotics. Let's look at some of the most common.

AVOID ENVIRONMENTAL TOXINS

Environmental toxins have a profound effect on our bodies, and it can be hard to recognize where they're coming from. This is by no means an exhaustive list of possible environmental toxins, but these are some of the exposures that commonly affect the gut.

Herbicides

Plenty of people think they're doing the right thing for their gut by eating salads every day, but if they're eating foods that aren't organic, those leafy greens might have glyphosate on them (the active ingredient in Roundup), which is an antimicrobial used to kill weeds. Not surprisingly, it also kills good microbes in the stomach. Glyphosate can influence dopamine and serotonin metabolism and depletes manganese, which is essential for certain genes to function and protect our mitochondria.[9] We recommend eating organic foods whenever possible.

---

9   Yassine Ait Bali, Saadia Ba-Mhamed and Mohamed Bennis, "Behavioral and Immunohistochemical Study of the Effects of Subchronic and Chronic Exposure to Glyphosate in Mice," *Frontiers in Behavioral Neuroscience* 11 (2017): 146.

The Environmental Working Group puts out a "dirty dozen" list yearly,[10] exposing the most toxic foods that are grown conventionally. When it's feasible, parents should stick to that list for buying organic produce and skip the food if they cannot access it. For example, since strawberries are so porous, they soak up the toxins that cannot be washed off. People eating nonorganic strawberries are also getting a dose of toxicity with that ingestion.

Chlorine

A lot of people don't think about the chlorine that's in water systems. Chlorine can kill off beneficial bacteria just as much as an antibiotic does (especially since we get exposure to it daily). A daily dose of fluoride, lead, and chemicals in the water can do a lot more harm to the gut if it's ingested throughout the day. We recommend consuming healthy, filtered water at home. People should avoid plastic bottles when they can and drink out of glass or stainless steel (to avoid chemicals leached from plastics, which can increase toxicity in the body). While a full-house reverse osmosis system might be a little expensive to install, it's often worthwhile. An alternative is to obtain a good filtered water system for the sink or keep one in the fridge.

---

10 "Dirty Dozen: EWG's 2018 Shopper's Guide to Pesticides in Produce," Environmental Working Group, https://www.ewg.org/foodnews/dirty-dozen.php.

Arsenic

Arsenic exposure can disrupt the gut microbiome and the ability to detox properly.[11] We had one patient who lived on a farm and lived what seemed to be an ideal, healthy life, but she had sky-high levels of arsenic. Her mother didn't clean with chemicals, was extremely particular about anything potentially being toxic, and the girl's diet consisted of only organic plants and grass-fed and free-range meats. She also drank goat's milk (and ate fermented goat yogurt) straight from the goat in their pasture. We couldn't figure it out for the longest time, but when we learned that the goat was drinking out of a well on their property that contained traces of arsenic in it, we had our answer. The goat was passing arsenic through its milk, slowly adding to this vulnerable child's toxic load.

Municipal Compost

Another seemingly healthy product that can cause problems is compost. Some cities use municipal compost, a biosolid from primary and secondary waste-activated sludge from the city's wastewater plant. It makes plants flourish but, unfortunately, can have fecal matter from humans in it, which is likely to contain chemicals. When people plant vegetables using the compost, those chemicals can make it into the plants they eat, and thus, the gut.

---

11   Xiaoxi Dong et al., "Arsenic Exposure and Intestinal Microbiota in Children from Sirajdikhan, Bangladesh," *PLoS One* 12, no. 12 (December 6, 2017).

We've had a few patients that play in municipal compost and end up with horrible outbreaks of hives and eczema. Another vote for using compost created in the kitchen!

CONSIDER SUPPLEMENTS

Nutritional supplements can help heal the gut. Again, there's no one-size-fits-all solution, but here are some of the supplements we frequently use in our practice.

Colostrum

If we see a child with diarrhea several times a day, we don't hesitate initiating colostrum as first line therapy. Colostrum, or immunoglobulin (often from bovine or egg sources), is very healing for the gut lining.[12] We prefer a specific brand called EnteraGam because it has many studies behind it that show it lessens episodes of loose stool in IBD patients.[13] While EnteraGam is a prescription medical food (a fancy way to say that pharmaceutical companies have gotten hold of naturally occurring products) immunoglobulin support products can be purchased from other supplement sources.

---

12 M. Halasa et al., "Oral Supplementation with Bovine Colostrum Decreases Intestinal Permeability and Stool Concentrations of Zonulin in Athletes," *Nutrients* 9, no. 4 (April 8, 2017).

13 H.S. Odes and Z. Madar, "A Double-Blind Trial of a Celandin, Aloevera and Psyllium Laxative Preparation in Adult Patients with Constipation," *Digestion* 49, no. 2 (1991): 65-71.

Magnesium Citrate and Aloe Vera Juice

Conversely, if a patient is having chronic constipation, we will start them on magnesium citrate or aloe before even testing.[14] Aloe's anthraquinones stimulate peristalsis (contractions) in the gut, so it's helpful for getting short-term results when needed. Sometimes we need an immediate solution, then we can take our time in figuring out why constipation is persistent. We have had patients who have had such severe constipation in the past they have had bowel blockages or even had to have a bowel resection surgery. Constipation comes from not adequately taking the trash out on a daily basis. Miralax, often used by pediatricians and GI doctors, can help clear the bowel by drawing water into the gut. While this might be an effective tool, we feel cautious about using it long term since it contains PEG 3350, which has been reported to cause psychiatric changes in some children. The Children's Hospital of Philadelphia has been conducting a study on these changes and should be releasing their findings soon.

Glutamine

Glutamine is another compound that helps heal the lining of the gut, serving as more of a Band-Aid for the GI lining.

---

14   A.F. Walker et al., " Mg Citrate Found More Bioavailable than

other Mg Preparations in a Randomised, Double-Blind Study. *Magnesium Research* 16, no. 3 (September 2003): 183–91.

It can help improve IBS diarrhea by balancing out mucus production. L-Glutamine is an essential amino acid that heals leaky guts, but it's not right for everyone. It appears to raise glutamate levels in some patients, which can increase hyperactivity and stimming in autism. It will have a stimulatory effect on the nervous system for those patients with problems with glutamine conversion.[15] A lot of our patients already have too much glutamate, and we may not know the status of their glutamic acid decarboxylase (GAD1) genes, and if it is mutated, that patient may have an even harder time converting glutamate, leading to excess. As a result, we don't use it frequently.

Zinc

Zinc has been strongly linked with reducing diarrhea in children that are malnourished. Usually, children with autism have some degree of malnourishment. Zinc is incredibly useful for reducing severity and duration of diarrhea.[16] It has also been known to tighten leaky gut junctions, specifically in Crohn's disease. It's known as a healing nutrient for the gut, but it's also really important for the immune system. As an added bonus, zinc can also really help increase appetite with picky eaters.

---

15   "GABA and Glycine," in D. Purves et al., eds., *Neuroscience* (Sunderland, MA: Sinauer Associates, 2001).

16   Chaitali Bajait and Vijay Thawani, "Role of Zinc in Pediatric Diarrhea," *Indian Journal of Pharmacology* 43, no. 3 (May-June 2011): 232-235; E. Lionetti et al., "Gluten Psychosis: Confirmation of a New Clinical Entity," *Nutrients* 7, no. 7 (2015).

Peppermint

Peppermint can reduce abdominal pain, flatulence, distension, and bowel frequency in patients with IBS. It has also demonstrated efficacy in reduction of post-op nausea and other nausea-related conditions. Peppermint is another reinoculation element for healing the gut lining.[17]

Omega-3 Fatty Acids

Omega-3 fatty acids help with many different things. They can help with inflammation, which can improve focus, anxiety, skin disorders, cognitive performance, and cardiovascular risk. Omega-3s can also have a positive impact on the microbiome. In 2017, a study looked at how omega-3 fatty acids affect gut microbiota.[18] They found the oils increased butyrate, a short-chain fatty acid that helps the gut lining. An increased butyrate level means a less inflamed gut. Butyrate even has potent regulatory effects on gene expression and can help lower oxidative stress.[19]

---

17 J.H. Liu et al., "Enteric-Coated Peppermint-Oil Capsules in the Treatment of Irritable Bowel Syndrome: A Prospective, Randomized Trial," *Journal of Gastroenterology* 32 (1997):765–8.

18 L. Costantini et al., "Impact of Omega-3 Fatty Acids on the Gut Microbiota," *International Journal of Molecular Sciences* 18, no. 12 (December 7, 2017).

19 R.B. Canani et al., A. "Potential Beneficial Effects of Butyrate in Intestinal and Extraintestinal Diseases," *World Journal of Gastroenterology* 17, no. 12 (March 28, 2011): 1519–28.

Enzymes

Digestion often gets disrupted in children with autism, who seem to inhale their food, whether because of issues with texture or because they won't sit quietly to eat, often running around with food in a tantrum, so the digestion process gets disrupted. We secrete enzymes when we chew, and this starts the process of digestion: breaking down carbohydrates, fats, and proteins. Children who take two bites and swallow won't have as many enzymes. We encourage parents to do whatever they can to slow down dinner time, as their child needs to be in a state of "resting" to get their bodies in an optimal state of digesting. We also suggest they avoid drinking too many liquids during big meals so the enzymes don't get diluted. This can help the digestion process more than any pill.

One way a parent can recognize if their child is lacking enzymes for fat is that their stools will float or will appear greasy. It's a telltale sign of fatty acid malabsorption within stool. Different enzymes break down different foods. Some supplement enzymes can help break down gluten, but we rarely recommend them because it's too tempting to take the pill and still eat the pizza that's causing the problem. That won't balance the gut.

IN DEFENSE OF SUPPLEMENTS

A lot of people get misinformation on supplements from their providers, who may dismiss supplements as lacking in evidence. We think it's important for our patients—and our readers—to know that everything we use is backed by plenty of evidence.

Many supplements have been studied and found effective, although the public may not know as much about them because these studies lack pharmaceutical industry sponsors. Sometimes studies on new "medicines" are really studies on supplements, such as the prescription medication Deplin, which is essentially fifteen milligrams of methyl folate.

We study the supplements we recommend, and when we endorse a brand, it's because a third party has tested and endorsed the product for potency, purity, and quality. Because supplements are regulated as a food in the United States, not a medication, there are lots of supplements on the shelf with no quality guarantee. We only use products that have third-party-product testing and verification, such as GMP-C or the National Sanitation Foundation. It's part of how we are able to do what we do, but we never put anyone on anything they don't need. In fact, we usually trim down the number of products people take when they come to see us for the first time.

Sometimes, supplements are the only choice. Some patients' families have trouble getting their child to eat a pound of broccoli a day. We get that. It's astounding how many patients come to us overweight and overfed, yet they are very undernourished. These patients are in need of vitamin and mineral support. Just because someone is overweight does not mean their body has too many of the *right* nutrients on board. To have optimal health, they need the right dosing of a nutrient, in the right form, with the right timing, by the right route (which sometimes means injectable, or absorption that happens under the tongue or through the skin).

Balance in the gut obviously depends on the kinds of foods a person ingests but not always in the most obvious of ways. A lot of patients with SIBO (small intestine bacterial overgrowth), for instance, have something called hypochlorhydria. This deficiency of hydrochloric acid leads to an overgrowth of bacteria in the wrong portion of the gut. When the small intestine is imbalanced, microbes have a heyday with foods high in short-chain carbohydrates. They ferment and off-gas methane, which causes gas and bloating, so even seemingly healthy foods can cause symptoms of dysbiosis.

Nonetheless, there are several foods that have been proven to help bring the gut back into balance. We'll explore a few here.

Bone Broth

Bone broth is rich in minerals and amino acids that can help heal the gut. It contains collagen and glutamine in a natural form that can repair the gut lining. Bone broth also contains lycine, proline, and tryptophan, which help reduce inflammation in the gut. It really is true that chicken noodle soup can help people get better faster.[20]

---

20 Victor Chedid et al., "Herbal Therapy Is Equivalent to Rifaximin for the Treatment of Small Intestinal Bacterial Overgrowth," *Global Advances in Health and Medicine* 3, no. 3 (May 2014): 16–24.

Parents can often make bone broth, freeze a portion, and allow their children to drink it twice a week. Giving it to them at night can even help with sleep.[21] (We caution against frequent intake of bone broth in our patients who have a hard time with high histamine foods. Bone broth historically is high in histamines.)

Probiotics and Prebiotics

Studies of prebiotics and probiotics continue to show that they're safe and effective. Among the common species you can find over the counter are lactobacillus, bifidobacterium, and saccharomyces boulardii. Amongst several other pharmaceutical-grade probiotics, we have had good results with VSL 3, an over-the-counter probiotic (that has 125 billion colony-forming units of bacteria per capsule). It has the most evidence supporting its use, and it's very safe to take.[22] When parents cannot easily access other probiotic brands, this is a good one that is available at most drug stores.

It's important to note that simply introducing a probiotic is rarely sufficient, because probiotics will rarely stick around unless they have something to feed on. That's

---

21 B.O. Rennard et al., "Chicken Soup Inhibits Neutrophil Chemotaxis In Vitro," *Chest* 118, no.4 (October 2000): 1150–57.

22 J. Kim et al., "A Randomized Controlled Trial of a Probiotic, VSL#3, on Gut Transit and Symptoms in Diarrhoea-Predominant Irritable Bowel Syndrome," *Alimentary Pharmacology and Therapeutics* 17 (2003): 895–904.

why foods high in prebiotics are crucial, as well. Prebiotic foods include asparagus, bananas, dandelion greens, eggplants, endives, garlic, honey, artichokes, jicama, leeks, legumes, onions, peas, radicchio, whole grains, and yogurt.

Patients can do a lot more than just take a probiotic supplement, like gathering data on their responses to inflammatory foods, replacing enzymes, and altering bacteria levels. Some people who take the wrong probiotics—especially people with SIBO—may find their body just ferments them into gas. It's also important to consider the way some probiotic supplements are made. Some won't make it past the acidity of the gut. Not only is preparation of the probiotic important, but storage is as well. When buying probiotics online, you want to choose a company that can guarantee they are kept in a temperature-controlled environment. If probiotics get too hot, the active bacteria will die.

Fermented Foods

Fermented foods are incredibly useful because they can be both pre- and probiotics. When parents don't want to give probiotic supplements, we encourage them to increase fermented foods. There are whole grocery store sections of fermented foods, like kombucha, kimchi, and sauerkraut. Just about anything can be fermented. There are different strains of bacteria in all of these foods. In some cases, parents that can get their children eating fermented foods might mitigate the need to supplement with probiotics at all.

A great product to look into is kefir because it both replaces good bacteria and mitigates harmful yeast. The same applies to miso and tempeh. Yogurt can be both a pre- and probiotic. We just need to make sure it's plain and not loaded with sugar. If the child doesn't tolerate dairy, there are plenty of nondairy yogurts. Parents just need to be sure there are no added dyes or sugars and that it contains live and active cultures.

How do we get children to eat these foods, though? If we get patients young enough, we can encourage parents to adjust their child's diet each day, little by little. Jicama, for example, is an easy food to give to smaller children. It usually comes in little wedges that are easy for babies to pick up and chew on. Slightly older children can have an ounce or two of kombucha every day and try sauerkraut on their grilled meats or on eggs in the morning. There are even recipes for making jicama fries, which go over well with older children. Cook sauerkraut into eggs in the morning. Parents can even make their own yogurt using an Instapot, giving them control over the sugar and flavor that make it more appealing to children. There are ways to get fermented foods into children in ways they'll like.

THE TRUTH ABOUT AMAZON—FOUR THINGS EMILY AND JANA WANT YOU TO KNOW

While we are big proponents of supplements, we feel like it is our duty to warn our patients about buying them from Amazon. Here is a copy of an email we blasted to patients:

Amazon Prime is convenient, we're no fools. When you're needing a quick fix for whatever your need (like that fidget spinner your daughter just *has* to have), it is what most of us go to. But when it comes to buying your supplements from Amazon, there are some hidden dangers we just don't think people realize. As your healthcare providers, we felt it was our responsibility to get this message out to you. This is the truth of what happens before the supplements are delivered to your door:

1. **They are sold illegally**—Supplement companies have entire departments dedicated to identifying and banning people selling their products online. They are illegal because the supplement company cannot be responsible for their quality or authenticity. Supplement companies even make you sign a legal document (when you sign up as a practitioner to sell them in your clinic) assuring that you will NOT sell them to Amazon. They know it's unsafe, and they are trying to protect their product's reputation.

2. **The expiration date can be altered**—If a practitioner cannot sell a product in their clinic, and it's close to expiration, many of them load it on Amazon to get rid of product so they don't realize a financial loss. Expiration dates can be altered, so what you are really getting is an expired product, or one that has sat for a long time and is near expiration.

3. **The product may be counterfeit**—Even though the bottle looks the same, is sealed the same, there is no

guarantee that the seller of that bottle (which could be anyone, including a scam artist) has not filled the product with capsules full of rice flour (or any other substance that does not look suspicious).

4. **The environmental quality (heat especially) has not been controlled**—This means your expensive probiotics could be killed in the heat, rendering them useless, or other ingredients (that needed temperature control to remain active) are now inactive from negligent environmental control.

In our years of experience, we have seen these things happen over and over again in our practice. Supplements can be very effective in helping manage disease or maintaining health, but not when those products are poor quality or counterfeit. We buy them from GMP-certified manufacturers, take excellent care of them in our office, and then we can ship them to you when you are ready. In the end, we just want you and your family to consume the highest quality of supplements you can so that those tools can support you as they are intended to on your journey to optimal wellness.

CONSIDER MEDICATIONS

While lifestyle choices can make a huge difference in a patient's health, sometimes we also use more conventional medications. Here's a quick look at some of the most common.

Antifungals

Yeast is one of the most common pathogens in patients with autism. Everyone has a certain level of yeast, but children with autism seem to have a harder time being burdened with it. We may try to treat it with diet, but frequently we end up chasing it around because it returns. In those cases, we may turn to prescription antifungals to treat yeast because it is much quicker.[23] We can often follow up our use of a prescription antifungal with herbal support to keep yeast from coming back.

One of our favorite products for patients on the antifungal protocol is Biocidin. It's a product of Bio-Botanical Research, a combination of herbs that attack not only yeast but biofilms, bacteria, and viruses. It helps balance out the intestinal microbiome by inhibiting pathogenic organisms. It contains herbs like oregano, milk thistle, echinacea, goldenseal, grapeseed extract, garlic, black walnut, tea tree oil, and lavender oil. These are all really tough on yeast and bacteria. In extremely hard cases, we start with pharmaceuticals like Nystatin or Diflucan, and then follow it up with Biocidin. Historically, antifungals have gotten a bad reputation for inducing liver failure, but there are some out there like Diflucan and Nystatin that can be used very safely in children.[24]

---

23   H. Santelmann et al., "Effectiveness of Nystatin in Polysymptomatic Patients: A Randomized, Double-Blind Trial with Nystatin versus Placebo in General Practice," *Family Practice* 18, no. 3 (June 2001): 258–265.

24   X. Lyu et al., "Efficacy of Nystatin for the Treatment of Oral Candidiasis: A Systematic Review and Meta-Analysis," *Drug Design, Development and Therapy* 10 (March 2016): 1161-71; O. Egunsola et al., "Safety of Fluconazole in Paediatrics: A Systemic Review," *European Journal of Clinical Pharmacology* 69, no. 6 (June 2013): 1211-21.

Which prescription medications we prescribe depends on symptoms and the results of preliminary tests. There are a lot of choices. We can use antiparasitics, antifungals, or certain antibacterial agents, if needed.

In this chapter, we've looked at many of the factors affecting the gut—what goes into it, stress levels, the amount of sleep, the environment, foods, supplements, and medications. What's important for parents to realize is that the gut is central to health and that there are plenty of things that can be done to balance it. When it comes to rebalancing the gut, we have to remove what is not intended (certain foods and dysbiotic organisms), replace what is (such as pre- and probiotics, hydrochloride, and enzymes), and continue to be proactive with maintaining the balance achieved by avoiding known disrupting triggers (avoiding antibiotics when feasible, drinking chlorine-free water, eating foods that help healthy micro-organisms thrive). Each step gets us further down the road to improving health.

CHAPTER FIVE

IMMUNE TUNNELS

No road trip would be complete without driving through a tunnel or two. Sometimes we have to go "underground" to really understand what's going on. The immune system is a little like that—it's made up of many different elements, like bone marrow, white blood cells, and the lymphatic system, that we don't see until we dig a bit deeper.

The immune system can affect behavior significantly, especially in small children. When adults get the flu or a stomach bug, they're never at their happiest. They're tired and often feel depressed. The same thing happens in children, only it can be magnified. They may seem particularly cranky, even if the more obvious signs of infection, like fever, aren't present.

Children on the spectrum have significant burdens in their immune systems because, as we have learned in previous chapters, they often have multiple areas of inflammatory stress. The immune system's primary goal is to help us tolerate influences from the outside world. Inflammation is a programmed immune response, but sometimes, the body either responds too strongly to inflammation or doesn't respond strongly enough. Immune activation can also happen from "occult," or hidden, infections, where a child might not display the typical signs of illness, but there is an inflammatory burden from an invading organism. Many problems can remain hidden in these "tunnels" unless we know where to look.

IMMUNITY AND INFLAMMATION

When our younger patients ask about the immune system, we tell them that it's like an army inside our bodies fighting a battle for us. This army makes sure we can fight the bad guys, known as infections, viruses, parasites, and environmental toxicity. It helps us build tolerance through exposure to the chaos of the outside world.

A properly functioning immune system can keep us from getting sick. For example, when we were working in primary care, we both treated a ton of flu cases each season. One flu season, Emily was seeing an acutely ill patient, and while she was examining his throat, he coughed and sprayed mucus all over her face and even into her mouth. Emily's immune system was strong. She did not come down with the flu. In fact, that particular year almost every provider in her practice had to take sick leave, but she was able to see child after child and remained well. Her immune system was strong, and tolerant, despite the virulence of the influenza virus that she clearly had heavy exposure to.

On the other hand, not getting sick isn't always a good sign. We sometimes hear parents say their child never gets sick, which sounds good but might mean autoimmune dysfunction, especially as a small child. Getting "sick"—having a fever, for instance—is actually an appropriate immune response. Since there can be a lot of confusion on what an actual fever is, let us clarify—it is a temperature over 100.4 degrees Fahrenheit. The presence of a fever means our immune system is working, fighting, and creating an influx of helper molecules to eradicate whatever infection is going on. If a child never gets sick, it could be because the immune system doesn't know when to become active and put forth its front lines.

While fever can be a much-feared response by parents, when our patients get acutely ill, we *want* them to have a fever and often don't recommend treating it until it is at least over 101, preferably 102. Seizures from fevers are rare and only happen when the temperature gets extremely high, so letting the fever be present (as long as the child is able to stay hydrated and is not too lethargic) is optimal. If parents are going to treat a fever, we never recommend acetaminophen (Tylenol) in children older than four months, only ibuprofen (Motrin). Remember, a young infant (0–4 months) should always be seen by their provider within one day of fever. Older children can typically wait up to three days to be seen (if all other areas are stable). Acetaminophen is one of the primary causes of liver toxicity and depletes a critical nutrient called glutathione from the liver. This nutrient is imperative for detoxification (which we will cover later in the detox chapter) and one of the most critical nutrients in autism.[1] One of the worst mistakes parents unknowingly make is giving

---

1   W. Dröge and R. Breitkreutz, "Glutathione and Immune Function," *Proceedings of the Nutrition Society* 59, no. 4 (November 2000): 595–600.

acetaminophen after (or even before) vaccines. It blunts the fever immune response and impairs detoxification—two things that can work against the child, not for them.

Several factors contribute to hypersensitive immune systems, so we will investigate a patient's history and discuss issues that may have led to this deregulation. Often, we uncover a trigger that is then perpetuated by another source. That source is often inflammatory and sends the immune system into imbalance.

The first place we always look is—surprise!—the gut. The permeability of the gut is one of the first issues that leads to immune activation. Dr. Alessio Fasano, MD, pediatric gastroenterologist, researcher, and founder of the Center for Celiac Research, found that the intestinal epithelium (the cells lining the intestine) are bound together by a tight junction cement called zonulin. When an inflammatory trigger enters the gut, the zonulin breaks open, and particulate matter leaks through the intestinal wall into circulation. Immunoglobulins then attack the intruders and upregulate the immune system.[2]

Today there is increased interest in the functional medical community about the idea that this permeability also increases the incidence of toxic bacteria escaping from

2   Alessio Fasano, "Zonulin, Regulation of Tight Junctions, and Autoimmune Diseases," *Annals of the New York Academy of Sciences* 1258, no. 1 (July 2012): 25-33.

the gut into the body and causing a low-grade inflammatory state. This translocation is called endotoxemia, and researchers are discovering it plays a pivotal, even causal role, in autoimmune and related diseases.[3] When toxic bacteria in a person's blood is being fought off by their immune system, a process called molecular mimicry can occur. This means the immune system does not see the bacteria as something foreign, but rather, it starts to look at it as part of a person's self, and the body starts to attack itself, causing autoimmunity. For example, a pathogen known as proteus has been linked to rheumatoid arthritis.[4]

Lack of sleep and stress also contributes to permeability (or leaky gut). We now know that when there is a lot of stress, or catecholamine surges (epinephrine, dopamine, norepinephrine), it can stimulate harmful gram-negative bacteria to flourish.[5] If a child has problems with intestinal inflammation and an occult bacterial infection, and neither have been identified and treated, stressful triggers which cause more catecholamine chemicals can tip the child into a chronic disease state.

---

3   Karin de Punder and Leo Pruimboom, "Stress Induces Endotoxemia and Low-Grade Inflammation by Increasing Barrier Permeability," *Frontiers in Immunology*, 6 (2015): 223.

4   A. Ebringer and T. Rashid, "Rheumatoid Arthritis is an Autoimmune Disease Triggered by Proteus Urinary Tract Infection," *Clinical and Developmental Immunology* 13, no. 1 (March 2006): 41–48.

5   M.T. Bailey and C.L. Coe, "Maternal Separation Disrupts the Integrity of the Intestinal Microflora in Infant Rhesus Monkeys," *Developmental Psychobiology* 35, no. 2 (1999): 146–55.

PANDAS

We cannot discuss chronic immune activation and neglect to mention PANDAS, or pediatric autoimmune neuropsychiatric syndrome disorder associated with streptococcus. This "tunnel" takes many parents and physicians by surprise. It happens when a child is exposed to strep bacteria but does not exhibit any symptoms. Instead, he or she rapidly develops severe behavioral changes. Antibodies that should be fighting the bacteria start to attack the brain, causing encephalitis (or brain inflammation). Children who might qualify for this diagnosis go from being happy and easygoing to exhibiting extreme OCD, tics, separation anxiety, food restriction, aggression, and bed-wetting. Parents arrive in their child's pediatricians' offices saying, "My child has been replaced by someone else." Unfortunately, this is a commonly co-occurring condition we see in our autistic population, and it is not surprising based on the immune vulnerability that exists in the autistic community.

PANDAS is still very controversial in the medical community because there is not one test that confirms the diagnosis. It's a clinical diagnosis with room for interpretation based on the clinician that sees the patient. In addition, the diagnosis is now extended beyond strep (called PANS, or pediatric autoimmune neuropsychiatric syndrome) because infections such as Epstein-Barr, varicella, influenza, Lyme, and mycoplasma can also trigger this brain inflammation. It wasn't until Dr. Susan Swedo, MD, from the National Institutes of Health, published guidelines on how to test for, recognize, and treat PANDAS that it has started to gain acceptance.[6] Now, major universities are backing research and many children are getting better with antibiotics, antivirals, steroids, immunoglobulins, inflammatory support, and even nutraceutical support.

FOOD ALLERGY AND SENSITIVITY PANELS

One last major area that can cause immune hyper-sensitivity/reactivity is food allergies and sensitivities. Remember when we previously discussed how a leaky gut can cause autoimmune inflammation? Well, most of that matter leaking through the gut is undoubtedly food! With our patients, we often tell them it is similar to the story of "Which came first, the chicken or the egg?" Food allergies can cause intestinal inflammation, leading to more food allergies because the immune system is fighting foreign matter in the wrong place (like in the bloodstream, rather than being absorbed into the gut). Or there is a leaking gut due to other factors, such as unbalanced gut flora that has caused intestinal inflammation, which also will create

---

6   K. Chang et al., "Clinical Evaluation of Youth with Pediatric Acute-onset Neuropsychiatric Syndrome (PANS): Recommendations from the 2013 PANS Consensus Conference," *Journal of Child and Adolescent Psychopharmacology* 25, no. 1 (February 2015): 3–13.

a barrier disturbance for absorption and lead to foods leaking through and causing immune activation.[7]

When a patient has never had allergy or sensitivity testing, we recommend getting labs done. When we look at an IgE response, we're looking for an immediate response of the immune system to that food. This can happen relatively quickly—typically within the first hour—so it is relatively easy to see the response to a food. In fact, these are the allergies that traditional allergists look for, the IgE mediated response. It is immediate and could lead to a multisystem response of inflammation, also known as anaphylaxis (which could require an epinephrine pen to get under control).

The less traditional, but still very important, type of allergic response is called an IgG response (or delayed sensitivity, often found with leaky gut). It looks at delayed immune reactions that show up four to seventy-two hours after exposure. These responses don't lead to anaphylactic symptoms in a child, but they contribute to a buildup of inflammation over time and can exacerbate problems such as stomach pain, hives, eczema, insomnia, headache, constipation, or diarrhea.[8] Symptoms can be amplified

---

7   P.E. Brandtzaeg, "Current Understanding of Gastrointestinal Immunoregulation and Its Relation to Food Allergy," *Annals of the New York Academy of Sciences* 964 (May 2002): 13-45.

8   Kelly Dorfman, "IgG Allergies in Autism, ADHD, Asthma, Autoimmune and More," *Epidemic Answers* (August 18, 2013), https://epidemicanswers.org/igg-allergies-autism-adhd-asthma-autoimmune/

by what a child eats. If we can identify the allergen, we can then advise parents to take children off the offender indefinitely or, depending on how serious the reaction, reintroduce it after six months to see how they tolerate it.

For an IgG sensitivity panel, we recommend removing most of the foods the patient is regularly eating for twenty-one days.[9] After twenty-one days, they can reintroduce each food. We recommend giving each food at least three days, but up to a week, of its own. The child eats it a few times per day that week, and the parent monitors their reactions, looking for delayed symptoms: Did they have a bad week at school? Did they wake up more at night? Were they complaining about their stomach? Did their eczema flare up?

Some people doubt the usefulness of sensitivity panels, but there is plenty of research supporting them and the way the immune system reacts. The vast majority of our patients who do the sensitivity panel and elimination diet see some improvement.[10]

---

9   W. Atkinson et al., "Food Elimination Based on IgG Antibodies in Irritable Bowel Syndrome: A Randomised Controlled Trial," *Gut* 53, no. 10 (October 2004): 1459–64.

10   Mohammad Reza Khakzad et al., "The Evaluation of Food Allergy on Behavior in Autistic Children," *Reports of Biochemistry and Molecular Biology* 1, no. 1 (October 2012): 37–42.

IMMUNOGLOBULIN DEFICIENCIES

An underactive immune system can be just as harmful as an overactive one. Some children have innate immune issues rooted in immunoglobulin deficiencies they were born with or have developed after having a severe infection, such as Epstein-Barr. Immunoglobulins are a type of proteins, or antibodies, in the blood that help fight antigens such as viruses, bacteria, and toxins. Some children on the autism spectrum have these deficiencies, so if there is a history of chronic illnesses, such as lots of ear infections, upper respiratory infections, and frequent fevers, we might go down this path and make sure the child's blood levels are within normal range.[11]

We once had a patient, referred to us by a psychiatrist, who came in on six different psychiatric medications. The psychiatrist kept placing him on medication after medication because nothing was helping the child's psychiatric symptoms. It turned out the child had an immunoglobulin deficiency (called hypogammaglobulinemia), and the primary source of his symptoms was his immune deficiency. Once this child started receiving therapy with intravenous immunoglobulin therapy (IVIG), we were able to slowly wean him off his psychiatric medications. By taking into account how all his biological systems were

---

11   L. Heuer et al., "Reduced Levels of Immunoglobulin in Children with Autism Correlates with Behavioral Symptoms," *Autism Research* 1, no. 5 (October 2008): 275-83.

connected, we were able to discover the root cause of his illness, and now he is thriving.

MITOCHONDRIAL HEALTH

Why are we talking about mitochondria in our immune chapter? Because mitochondria play an especially critical role in immune health. In fact, the mitochondria are responsible for establishing types of immune cells and regulating their function.[12] Mitochondria are the powerhouses of the body. These tiny structures exist in nearly every cell in the body. They generate adenosine triphosphate (ATP), the fuel that drives all of the body's functions.[13] The mitochondria as conductors of an orchestra, where instead of cueing violins, they instruct organelles within the cell, such as lysosomes, to go detoxify this or that chemical.[14] In autism, there are a lot of issues with low mitochondrial output, or myopathies, stemming from many factors, including genetic predisposition, nutritional deficiencies, and burden on cells.

There are more mitochondria within the brain and musculoskeletal tissue than anywhere else in the body.

---

12   S.E. Weinberg, L.A. Sena, and N.S. Chandel, "Mitochondria in the Regulation of Innate and Adaptive Immunity," *Immunity* 42, no. 3 (March 17, 2015): 406–417.

13   Suzanne Goh, "Autism and Mitochondrial Function: Testing and Treatments," *Talking About Curing Autism*, https://tacanow.org/family-resources/autism-and-mitochondrial-function/.

14   Kiran Todkar, Hema S. Ilamathi, and Marc Germain, "Organelles Within the Cell Such as Lysosomes, *Frontiers in Cell and Developmental Biology* 5 (2017): 106.

Mitochondria need a lot of key nutrients to function properly. They particularly rely on two major sources of fuel, heme (or iron) and essential fatty acids. Carnitine is the shuttle that gets fatty acids through the lipid membrane of the cell and feeds the mitochondria. That mitochondrial respiratory chain is like a factory pumping out ATP. To work properly, it needs micronutrients such as NADH, coenzyme Q10 (ubiquinone), methyl folate, vitamin E, and L-carnitine. Nicotinamide adenine dinucleotide (NAD) functions as a cofactor in over 200 cellular reactions.[15]

That sounds complicated, but the key concept is that to produce energy, mitochondria rely on a chain of inputs. When the chain is working efficiently, it produces adequate adenosine triphosphate, our energy molecules.

Literature suggests nearly every child on the spectrum has some type of mitochondrial pathology.[16] It has long been difficult to diagnose because testing has been complex and only available with access to a specialist. (Patients usually need to visit specialists and undergo a muscle biopsy and an MRI, along with a host of other

---

15   Joseph Pizzorno, "Mitochondria—Fundamental to Life and Health," *Integrative Medicine: A Clinician's Journal* 13, no. 2 (April 2014): 8–15.

16   K.K. Griffiths and R.J. Levy, "Evidence of Mitochondrial Dysfunction in Autism: Biochemical Links, Genetic-Based Associations, and Non-Energy-Related Mechanisms," *Oxidative Medicine and Cellular Longevity* (2017); Jacqueline R. Weissman et al., "Mitochondrial Disease in Autism Spectrum Disorder Patients: A Cohort Analysis," *PLoS One* 3, no. 11 (2008).

blood tests.) Now, MitoSwab has developed a buccal (cheek) swab test that is 84 percent correlated with the muscle biopsy and much less painful and invasive.[17] We have used this test in our office and seen improvements when treating patients with specific mito support.

When we see a child with poor growth and muscle tone who cannot tolerate any exercise, or has difficulty chewing or swallowing food, or exhibits abnormal movement disorders, we have to consider mitochondrial disorder. Most times, it's not mitochondrial disorder, but mitochondrial dysfunction.

Mitochondrial dysfunction can be triggered by genetic predispositions and shortages of vitamin cofactors.[18] Children with mitochondrial dysfunction are not getting all the fuel they need. That's why they have low energy and poor muscle tone, get sick often, and often need occupational or physical therapy very early on. They feel tired a lot and have exercise intolerance. These are the children who would rather sit than play. Oftentimes, they'll have feeding difficulties too.

This is why "mito cocktails" are so important to patient

---

17   http://mitoswab.com

18   Richard I. Kelley, "Evaluation and Treatment of Patients with Autism and Mitochondrial Disease," *Kennedy Krieger Institute*, http://mitomedical.com/wp-content/uploads/2013/04/Dr.-Richard-Kelly-Autism_Mitochondrial_Disease11.pdf.

health. Dr. Richard Kelley at Johns Hopkins has a mitochondrial protocol for children with suspected mitochondrial myopathies or mitochondrial dysfunction in autism.[19] In his work, he has identified that autistic children often need significant doses of mitochondrial nutrient cofactors, and when these are replaced via supplementation, over time, there is typically tremendous developmental and neurological benefit.[20]

Another promising supplement in mitochondrial health is nicotinamide riboside. It increases mitochondrial biogenesis and NAD levels, which are both helpful in making the mitochondria more dense in number and robust in function. It provides neurological, metabolic, and methyl endurance support.[21]

Nutrients that support the mitochondria can have a far-reaching effect on growth and development. These nutrients are not an overnight fix, however. Parents and providers who target mitochondrial support for their children need to give the therapy consistently, and for

19 Richard I. Kelley, "Evaluation and Treatment of Patients with Autism and Mitochondrial Disease," *Kennedy Krieger Institute*, June 13, 2009.

20 Richard I. Kelley, "Evaluation and Treatment of Patients with Autism and Mitochondrial Disease!" http://mitomedical.com/wp-content/uploads/2013/04/Dr.-Richard-Kelly-Autism_Mitochondrial_Disease11.pdf

21 Garth L. Nicolson, "Mitochondrial Dysfunction and Chronic Disease: Treatment with Natural Supplements," *Integrative Medicine: A Clinician's Journal* 13, no. 4 (August 2014): 34-43.

many months, to see improvements. They come slowly, but they will come for those that need them.

NONSPECIFIC AUTOIMMUNITY

Autoimmunity means there is an immune abnormality; however, doctors may never find exactly what that abnormality is, because many children with autism have nonspecific positive autoimmune markers called antinuclear antibodies (or ANA).[22] We recently saw an eight-year-old girl who came to us with symptoms of aggression, oppositional behavior, and episodes of frequent rage. After conducting blood work, we found she had some occult infections she was struggling with (such as mycoplasma) and her ANA was very high. After treating her infections and optimizing her through functional medicine, within nine months, her ANA was no longer positive. She is also back to her happy-go-lucky self, back at school this year, thriving without any behavioral issues. Immune dysfunctions in children on the spectrum are multifaceted. Genetics certainly play a role, and now newer evidence is also illuminating a mother's immunity may play a role as well.[23]

---

22 G.A. Mostafa and N. Kitchener, "Serum Anti-Nuclear Antibodies as a Marker of Autoimmunity in Egyptian Autistic Children," *Pediatric Neurology* 40, no. 2 (February 2009): 107-12.

23 Elizabeth Edmiston, Paul Ashwood, and Judy Van de Water, "Autoimmunity, Autoantibodies, and Autism Spectrum Disorder," *Biological Psychiatry* 81, no. 5 (March 1, 2017): 383-390.

One solution for nonspecific autoimmunity is a drug called low-dose naltrexone (or LDN). LDN is a short-term opioid blocker, and when opioids are blocked, the body responds by producing more natural opioids, called endorphins, which in turn stimulate positive immune effects. In children on the spectrum, this drug has been used in a variety of doses and appears safe and well tolerated.[24] While the majority of the studies are for behavioral stability and regulation, LDN is used widely across many autoimmune diseases, and for children on the spectrum with autoimmune challenges, it may be a medication choice that is effective for multiple purposes.

ILLUMINATING THE TUNNELS

We have learned about immunity, and still it seems like a complex topic. Indeed, it is. Families can feel lost in these tunnels, like they are navigating around in the dark, looking for their way to the surface.

Immunity in autism is an advanced topic for even clinicians to discuss. Parents need to understand their child's immune system is about more than just getting a fever. Immune stress can come from the mitochondria, gut,

---

24   C.A. Doyle and C.J. McDougle, "Pharmacotherapy to Control Behavioral Symptoms in Children with Autism," *Expert Opinion on Pharmacotherapy* 13, no. 11 (August 2012): 1615–29.

infections, the food a child is eating, and more.[25] As we go down these tunnels, they tend to branch off into even more tunnels.

Our job is to shine a light on the hidden passages. There are a number of tests that can help us do that. Because one system imbalance can cause other systems to react and become out of balance as well, we are going to list below the most common labs we use in our practice (addressing the five core areas of imbalance discussed in this book).

- Serum labs: CBC, CMP, TSH, Free T4, Free T3, Homocysteine, Iron/IBC, Ferritin, HsCRP, ANA, Lipid panel, MMA, RBC Folate, RBC Zinc, glutathione, acetylcarnitine profile, plasma amino acids, essential fatty acid profile, lead, mercury, aluminum, arsenic, IgE food panels, vitamin D, immunoglobulin panel (IgG, IgA, IgG, IgE)
- GI map
- Candida panel
- IgG food sensitivities
- Organic acids
- Comprehensive stool analysis (with parasitology)
- Hair metal testing

---

25 D.A. Rossignol and R.E. Frye, "A Review of Research Trends in Physiological Abnormalities in Autism Spectrum Disorders: Immune Dysregulation, Inflammation, Oxidative Stress, Mitochondrial Dysfunction and Environmental Toxicant Exposures," *Molecular Psychiatry* 17, no. 4 (April 2012): 389–401.

- Celiac disease panel
- Gluten and casein peptides
- Urinary essential elements
- Urinary toxin profile
- Environmental toxin profile
- Mycotoxin profile
- MitoSwab
- Developmental genetic panel
- Methylation genetic panel
- Urine porphyrins

A selection is offered on our website (NeuronutritionAssociates.com). We encourage you to review your choices with a practitioner.

CHAPTER SIX

TOXICITY TURN

Most drivers have gotten stuck behind an overladen truck trying to make it up a steep hill. The truck's engine works harder and harder as it approaches the peak, and the truck goes slower and slower. On the other hand, a truck with a light load can be very efficient, reaching the summit in no time. Many of us operate like the first truck.

We're overloaded with a toxic burden that keeps us from optimum health. If we can be more like the second truck, we can make it further down the road much faster. There is evidence that children on the autism spectrum have greater burdens of toxicity and oxidative stress, so in essence, their loads are heavy.[1]

Unfortunately, we often lack accurate information about what we are putting into our bodies and our children's bodies. Some parents think that because they do not vaccinate their children, their child isn't exposed to toxins. This just isn't true. We had a patient who wasn't vaccinated, but when we did a heavy metal test, the child's mercury levels were astronomical. We accumulate toxins that we encounter in daily life, such as products we use on our skin. Our houses can even be a source of toxins, especially if there is mold and water damage. The air in our homes is generally more toxic than the air outside. Schools and therapy centers can contain toxins. What is a child exposed to if they spend forty hours a week in a specific place? What's that environment like?

WHAT IS A TOXIN?

We define a toxin as anything that can make it into the

---

1   J.K. Kern and A.M. Jones, "Evidence of Toxicity, Oxidative Stress, and Neuronal Insult in Autism," *Journal of Toxicology and Environmental Health Part B* 9, no. 6 (November–December 2006): 485–99.

body and disrupt homeostasis. These disruptions can come in the shape of pesticides on our food, chemicals in our sunscreen, heavy metals found in old plumbing pipes, or air quality in a child's environment. A toxin is any foreign invader that disrupts biochemical processes within the body. At a high enough dose, anything can become a toxin. For example, taking zinc can be beneficial for detoxification, but at extremely high doses, it becomes a toxin. Another example is arsenic. It is used in rice farming to keep rodents from eating the rice on the way to the mill (which is why we always recommend spending the extra money for organic rice). If a child is eating a lot of rice, he can become toxic from high levels of arsenic. Studies have shown arsenic exposure can disrupt the gut microbiome and the ability to properly detox.[2]

EVERYDAY EXPOSURE

We encounter some patients who use conventional personal care products every day and think they're safe because they are applied topically, or only used in the hair. These people are still susceptible to toxic accumulation, though. Small doses of the chemicals in these products might be okay, but anything used multiple times

---

2   K. Lu et al., "Arsenic Exposure Perturbs the Gut Microbiome and its Metabolic Profile in Mice: An Integrated Metagenomics and Metabolomics Analysis," *Environmental Health Perspectives* 122, no. 3 (March 2014): 284–91.

a day, 365 days a year, will inevitably accumulate until it becomes significant.

The overall accumulation of toxins also makes a significant difference in how people react to them. As populations grow and people move to city centers, they tend to get exposed to more pollution and ingest more toxins. The rates of autism in areas where air pollution is a huge problem, such as China, are among the highest in the world. In the United States, approximately 96 percent of products are made using synthetic chemicals. These chemicals are in our clothes, our furniture, anything we eat, and anything made in a factory, such as pottery and cookware.

The CDC began measuring human exposure to chemicals back in 1976. For forty-one years, they measured them but didn't do anything about it. Now, we are beginning to see the emergence of safer products. Our intention is not to scare people into never going outside again. We can still sleep on our mattresses, breathe the air in our homes, and put on makeup. We just want people to be mindful of toxins and make the least toxic choice whenever possible.

THE DETOX PROCESS

It's nearly impossible to avoid all exposure to toxins. Fortunately, our bodies are made to detoxify. When a toxin enters our body, we normally go through several phases of detox. In phase one, the liver begins by opening up the toxin, destroying it, hydrolyzing it, and breaking it apart. Once the toxin is taken apart, it becomes a free radical, or reactive oxygen species. If the reactive oxygen species binds to tissue and DNA, it can damage the body (like an internal rusting), so our bodies try to bind them up in the second phase. Phase two of detox uses processes of binding, such as sulfation, glucuronidation, and conjugation. After they are bound, we can move to phase three of detox, which is excretion, and we get rid of them in our urine, bile, and sweat.

All these processes are aided by specific nutrients and bodily elimination processes. Unfortunately, many kids don't have lifestyles that support these processes. A lot of children sit in front of the TV, they're constipated, they don't go outside and sweat, and they don't eat the right nutrients to assist with the phases of detox. As a result, we see high body burdens in a lot of our patients. That's why regular exercise and bowel movements are so helpful for our patients. We want a child's toxic load to be as low as possible. The lower the toxic load, the less inflammation and stress on the body and the brain. An empty truck goes uphill much faster than a full one!

Exposure to potentially harmful chemicals on a daily basis is virtually unavoidable. The majority of the 85,000 chemicals registered for production under the U.S. Toxic Substances Control Act (TSCA) were grandfathered in with little or no health and safety testing.[1] Medical conditions linked to toxic chemicals include obesity, metabolic syndrome, diabetes, cardiovascular disease, Alzheimer's and Parkinson's, cancers, and multisystem complaints such as fibromyalgia and multiple chemical sensitivities.[2]

Ten categories of toxic chemicals are known to be especially prevalent, persistent, and detrimental to human and environmental health:

1. heavy metals: lead (Pb), mercury (Hg), arsenic (As), cadmium (Cd), aluminum (Al)
2. polycyclic aromatic hydrocarbons (PAHs)
3. plastics (phthalates)
4. phenols, particularly bisphenol A (BPA)
5. organochloride pesticides (OCs)
6. organophosphate pesticides (OPs)
7. polychlorinated dibenzo-dioxin & furan (dioxins)
8. polychlorinated biphenyls (PCBs)
9. polybrominated diphenyl ethers (PBDEs)
10. polyfluorinated compounds (PFCs)

Reducing Dietary Exposures

1. Choose organic and low-fat or no-fat animal products such as dairy, eggs, meats (PAHs, OCs, OPs, dioxins, PCBs, PBDEs).
2. Choose cooking methods that are low-char and that allow animal fats to drip away, such as steaming (PAHs, OCs, OPs, dioxins, PCBs, PBDEs).
3. Consult local wildlife agencies before eating freshwater fish (PCBs, dioxins, PBDEs).
4. Never eat farmed salmon (PCBs), avoid eating larger carnivorous fish (Hg, PBDEs, PCBs) and use the Environmental Working Group (EWG) Good Seafood Guide.[3]
5. Use glass, ceramic, or stainless steel containers for heating and storing hot food (phthalates).
6. Avoid plastic water bottles, travel mugs and bladder-style hydration reservoirs and do not wash plastic food or beverage containers under high heat (phthalates).
7. Avoid using vinyl cling wrap and only buy canned foods that are BPA-free (BPA).
8. Avoid high-fructose corn syrup and rice syrup (As) and processed foods containing BHT, BHA, benzoate, sulfites, and artificial colorings and sweeteners.
9. Choose local, seasonal, and organic produce whenever possible. Wash all fruits and vegetables using mild additive-free soap and clean water (OCs, OPs).
10. Choose organic versions of the EWG "Dirty Dozen" list of high-pesticide produce (OCs, OPs).[4]

Reducing Home & Office Exposures

1. Consult the EWG Drinking Water Database[5] and consider testing your water supply. Use a NSF-certified water filter if indicated (Pb, As, Cd, trihalomethane, atrazine, benzene, etc.).
2. Clear water that has been standing overnight out of plumbing lines in your home or office by flushing the toilet or letting the tap run for several minutes before pouring out tap water for consumption (Pb, other metals).
3. Filter shower water (chlorine, OCs), and avoid using new vinyl shower curtains (phthalates).
4. Filter air in your bedroom and office using filters, ionizers or plants[6] (airborne toxins).
5. Cover or replace older foam furniture and consider removing old carpets and padding (PBDEs).
6. Remove shoes you've worn outside when entering your home (OPs).
7. Clean up broken thermometers and fluorescent bulbs with gentle sweeping and wiping up with gloves and disposable materials. Do not vacuum (Hg).
8. Choose fragrance- and solvent-free detergents and cleaning agents (phthalates) and consult the EWG Guide to Healthy Cleaning.[7]
9. Avoid non-stick pots and pans and do not buy stain-resistant clothing, carpet or furniture (PCBs).
10. Avoid products made with particleboard or medium-density fiberboard (formaldehyde, solvents).
11. Remove or paint over older pressure-treated wood (As). Use low- or no-VOC (volatile organic compound) paints, glues, sealants, etc. in new construction (solvents).[8]
12. With new construction, consider "baking" out noxious fumes by vacating (people, plants and animals) and setting the house heat at maximum for 24-hour cycles followed by ventilation and rechecking for fumes (solvents and other toxic chemicals).

Reducing Health Care & Personal Care Exposures

1. For general wellness: Stay well hydrated and consume alcohol in moderation, if at all.
2. Avoid acetaminophen for pain relief (especially after alcohol), and avoid taking multiple over-the-counter and prescription drugs simultaneously.
3. Stop smoking and avoid second-hand smoke (Cd, PAHs).
4. Inquire about preservatives in flu shots and vaccines and chose ones without Thimerisol (Hg).
5. Choose unscented, fragrance-free personal care products (phalates), avoid antiperspirants and antacids (Al), and use the EWG Cosmetics Database.[9]
6. Choose composite over metallic dental fillings and be sure that your dentist follows all of the recommended IAOMT[10] procedures when removing silver fillings (Hg).
7. Avoid having two different metals (e.g., mercury and gold) in your mouth; this can create low-voltage electric currents, which accelerates metal degradation.

Reducing Work & Hobby Exposures

1. Identify your exposures by consulting MSDS data sheets for all chemicals you use (various toxins).
2. Wear and maintain all appropriate personal protective equipment and keep any work clothes that may have toxins on them separate from your home (various toxins).

References

1. U.S. Environmental Protection Agency: http://www.epa.gov/oppt/existingchemicals/pubs/tscainventory/basic.html
2. Sears ME, Genuis SJ. J Environ Public Health. 2012;2012:356798 http://dx.doi.org/10.1155/2012/356798
3. Environmental Working Group: www.ewg.org/research/ewgs-good-seafood-guide
4. Environmental Working Group: http://www.ewg.org/foodnews/list.php
5. Environmental Working Group: http://www.ewg.org/tap-water/
6. Claudio L. Environ Health Perspect. 2011 Oct; 119(10): a426-a427. http://ehp.niehs.nih.gov/119-a426/
7. Environmental Working Group: http://www.ewg.org/guides/cleaners
8. U.S. Green Building Council's Green Home Guide: http://greenhomeguide.com/
9. Environmental Working Group: http://www.ewg.org/skindeep/
10. International Academy of Oral Medicine and Toxicology: http://iaomt.org/safe-removal-amalgam-fillings/

Some children can coast through life exposed to a high level of toxins and do just fine. Children with autism may be exposed to the same amount of toxins as neurologically typical children but do not react the same way. In fact, a recent study showed higher levels of lead (and lower levels of manganese and zinc) in baby teeth of children on the spectrum.[3] Children with autism also can have dysfunctions in the way they detox. We will learn more about this in the genetics chapter, but keep in mind that in addition to the amount of exposure from toxins, the way the body eliminates them can also be affected by an individual's genetic makeup.

When we talk to parents about toxins, we acknowledge that addressing the issue can feel overwhelming. If their child has many exposures, where do they even start? We tell them they don't have to do it all at once. Instead, we encourage them to make one positive change every week if they can. One week, get a water purifier. The next, an air purifier. After that, focus on buying organic produce. Over time, everyone can make positive changes.

Other families are more eager than overwhelmed. These families come in ready to detox their child. We appreciate their commitment to get started, but we recommend making sure we have all the support we need in place first.

---

3   Manish Arora et al., "Fetal and Postnatal Metal Dysregulation in Autism," *Nature Communications* (2017): Article number 15493.

Often when we address some of the things that we have previously discussed, such as nutrition and the gut, the child's own ability to detox becomes much more efficient.

Detoxification can also be stressful on the child, so we always want to make sure their bodies are in optimal shape before we dive into this process. For example, we had one family come to us interested in detoxifying mercury from their son. The boy had severe sleep issues, eczema, and irritable bowels. We had to take a deeper look into these areas and give this child treatment for those problems first. When it was time to look for mercury toxicity (about five months later), the child had no markers of any toxicity and had started making developmental gains.

Detoxification can take many forms. Oftentimes, when we're detoxing with chelation, activated charcoal helps by binding up toxins that are floating around and eliminating metals quickly. High doses of molybdenum, which binds up toxins that are released when yeast is killed off, can have tremendous results for people who feel flu-like, fatigued, and achy when they treat yeast. Molybdenum binds to those toxins to help get them out of the body quicker.[4] Some of our children with PANDAS and PANS

4   F. Jurnak, "The Pivotal Role of Aldehyde Toxicity in Autism Spectrum Disorder: The Therapeutic Potential of Micronutrient Supplementation," *Nutrition and Metabolic Insights* 8, suppl. 1 (2015): 57-77.

respond exceptionally well to molybdenum because it is protective for people who have mitochondrial dysfunction.[5] We also look at pyroluria, a zinc and copper imbalance, because molybdenum can decrease copper without affecting zinc levels. A lot of our children have higher than normal copper levels in their system, so molybdenum does a lot of legwork.[6]

CURRENT VERSES PAST TOXIC EXPOSURES

It is important to understand the difference between current exposures to toxins, in particular with heavy metals, and past exposure. Current exposure means the child, within the last one to two months, had an exposure to a heavy metal. This is a serious situation, and the source of that metal needs to be eradicated immediately. For example, we have seen a lot of babies in our practice in the past six months that have had elevated lead levels. These families are living in new houses, with new pipes, new construction, and could not find any source of lead (teething rings, pottery, toys from foreign countries) no matter how hard they looked. It turns out it was in their baby food! *Consumer Reports* listed many companies

---

5   R. Hille, J. Hall and P. Basu, "The Mononuclear Molybdenum Enzymes," *Chemical Reviews* 114, no. 7 (2014): 3963-4038.

6   Z. Marelja, S. Leimkühler, and F. Missirlis, "Iron Sulfur and Molybdenum Cofactor Enzymes Regulate the *Drosophila* Life Cycle by Controlling Cell Metabolism," *Frontiers in Physiology* 9, no. 50 (February 14, 2018): 50.

that had lead contamination in their products.[7] This is
known as a current exposure, and once those families
stopped buying contaminated products, their babies'
levels went down.

Past exposure is what most parents with children on
the spectrum are most concerned about. Did the heavy
metals in vaccines cause my child's autism? Some children have a harder time detoxifying metals based on
their antioxidant status and their genetics. At this date in
history, the data is too inconclusive to draw finite conclu-
sions about vaccines being the cause of autism. As we've
learned in this book, there are many potential sources of
inflammatory stress in a child that is autistic. It very rarely
is just one causal factor. The cause of autism is complex
and multifactorial, and no researcher to date claims they
have the definitive answer (and we would feel cautious
if they did). We do not claim to know the answer as well,
but what we do know is that applying functional medicine to a child that has autism (and decreasing their body
burden) will often yield physiological, emotional, and
developmental improvements.

CHELATION AND DETOX

When we find that a child has a toxic burden, what is

---

7   Jesse Hirsch, "Heavy Metals in Baby Food: What You Need to Know," *Consumer Reports*
     (August 16, 2018).

next? Our first goal is to identify the particular burden. In a world filled with toxins, it can range from toxic foods to toxic metals. If it is an environmental toxin, such as mold, we want to eradicate the source of that mold and then work hard on having that child get higher levels of nutrients that support their detox, such as glutathione, and get that child sweating so they can start excreting the toxic mold. Glutathione is one of our bodies' most powerful antioxidants, and it is critical for phase one and two of the detox process. Glutathione reduces oxidative stress in the body and the brain and has shown numerous benefits in autism.[8]

Unfortunately, the scientific community does not yet agree on the best way to identify toxic burden. Possibilities include hair metal testing, urinary porphyrin testing, or provoked urine testing.[9] Provoked urine testing is likely the most controversial; however, some clinicians say it is the most accurate. Provoking a urine requires giving a detoxification agent (such as DMSA) and then collecting the urine for several hours afterward to evaluate the body's net retention.

Not surprisingly, methods for removing toxins from the

---

8   A. Ghanizadeh et al., "Glutathione-related Factors and Oxidative Stress in Autism, A Review," *Current Medical Chemistry* 19, no. 23 (2012): 4000-4005.

9   R. Nataf et al., "Porphyrinuria in Childhood Autistic Disorder: Implications for Environmental Toxicity," *Toxicology and Applied Pharmacology* 214, no. 2 (July 2006): 99-108.

body, such as chelation, also come with controversy. Many parents come to us asking about using chelation to draw toxins from their child's body. If a child has a high metal burden, we may consider it. Chelation therapy involves administering agents to pull heavy metals from the body. Chelation can involve using prescriptive agents, such as DMSA or EDTA, or nutraceutical agents, such as alpha lipoic acid and garlic. Chelation isn't a quick cure. It takes time. Every child handles chelation differently, and most do best on a low-dose, slow method of administration.

Additional natural supports we recommend for detoxification include exercise, infrared saunas, and getting more antioxidants through vegetables like broccoli and cabbage, which are high in sulforaphanes.[10] Particular nutraceuticals can also aid the process of detoxification. Turmeric (with 95 % curcuminoids and black pepper extract), phosphatidylcholine, methyl folate, B12, B6, NAC, and alpha lipoic acid can help support detoxification. Resveratrol can also facilitate detox, especially with arsenic.[11]

---

10 K. Singh et al., "Sulforaphane Treatment of Autism Spectrum Disorder (ASD)," *Proceedings of the National Academy of Sciences of the United States of America* 111, no. 43 (October 2014): 15550–55.

11 Zhigang Zhang et al., "Resveratrol, a Natural Antioxidant, Has a Protective Effect on Liver Injury Induced by Inorganic Arsenic Exposure," *BioMed Research International* (2014): 1-7.

CHELATION OPTIONS

DIMERCAPTOSUCCINIC ACID (DMSA)

Protocol Details

- DMSA is FDA approved for lead toxicity; for children age one and older give 20-30 mg/kg/day x 3 days, then stop for 11 days; cycle 6-8 rounds and then check metal levels.

Benefits

- Quick to mobilize and eliminate certain toxins; studies done on children three to eight years old received 3-6 rounds of DMSA and showed increased excretion of lead, mercury, antimony, and other metals.

Risks

- May cause an increase in yeast and side effects such as GI symptoms, adrenal fatigue, lowered white blood count, or stress on liver and kidneys (however these side effects are rare).

Labs Recommended

- DMSA provocation urine challenge testing; porphyrin testing or hair metal testing. Basic labs recommended to monitor liver and kidney function throughout therapy in addition to basic nutrients.

Support

- Essential minerals may also be chelated (with the metals) so monitoring iron and zinc is recommended. Other support includes NAC, glutathione, magnesium, garlic, curcumin, taurine, vitamin C, quercetin, and arginine (for lead).

TOPICAL DMSA/ALA
Protocol Details

- 5 mg/kg 3 x daily, applied for 3 days on/11 days off.

Benefits

- Bypasses gut absorption and may have less yeast symptoms/less side effects.

Risks

- Possible depletion of essential minerals which need to be monitored and repleted.

Labs Recommended

- Hair metal, urine, porphyrin, or blood test. Basic labs recommended to monitor liver and kidney function throughout therapy in addition to basic nutrients.

Support

- Vitamin C, vitamin E, magnesium, zinc, milk thistle, NAC, and adrenal cortex extract.

ANDY CUTLER CHELATION (ACC)

Protocol Details

- DMSA and/or ALA 1/8 mg per pound. 1/2 mg per pound every 3-4 hours for 72 hours; 5 days off. If a nighttime dose is missed by more than 30 minutes, the round must be stopped. If a daytime dose is missed by more than 1 hour, the round must be stopped.

Benefits

- Slow and more regimented dosing allows for less reabsorption of metals into tissues.

Risks

- Chelation can take between 100-300 rounds. ACC is a longer and slower process. Children might have a slight flare in symptoms 1-2 days after a round is completed. Negatives to ACC are interruption of sleep for the family, possible adrenal fatigue, increase in yeast, and lowered white blood cell count.

Labs Recommended

- Hair metal toxic elements with essential elements (counting rules); Porphyrin test to r/o mercury toxicity.

Support

- Vitamin C, vitamin E, magnesium, zinc, milk thistle, NAC, and adrenal cortex extract.

ETHYLENEDIAMINETETRAACETIC ACID (EDTA)

Protocol Details

- EDTA 500 -750 mg suppository, 1-3 x per week.

Benefits

- Efficient for lead and mercury removal. Typically less GI side effects or flares in yeast.

Risks

- EDTA can be dangerous when it is used while the patient has a current exposure to mercury. Once the mercury is bound in the body, it is very unlikely that EDTA would make it more toxic.

Labs Recommended

- Hair metal, urine, porphyrin, or blood test. Basic labs recommended to monitor liver and kidney function throughout therapy in addition to basic nutrients.

Support

- Vitamin C, vitamin E, magnesium, zinc, milk thistle, iron, NAC, and adrenal cortex extract.

NUTRACEUTICALS

Protocol Details

- Typically taken twice daily, for 3-6 months. Doses vary based on nutraceutical. All are over-the-counter and generally recognized as safe (GRAS rating). Strong evidence for detox with glutathione, NAC, allicin.

Benefits

- Slow, safe, over-the-counter, and no monitoring is typically needed.

Risks

- Risks are low; some GI upset when taken on empty stomach.

Labs Recommended

- Hair metal, urine, porphyrin, or blood test to evaluate metal burden. Repeat labs to monitor efficacy.

Support

- Ensure adequate elimination (such as no constipation or dehydration) while utilizing.

MODIFIED CITRUS PECTIN

Protocol Details

- 15 g MCP (Pectasol) in three divided doses daily for 2-4 weeks; additional protocols utilize for 3-6 months.

Benefits

- Modified alginates bind to heavy metals and environmental toxins within the digestive tract, preventing reabsorption into the bloodstream.

Risks

- Lack of double-blind studies that show prolonged use in children.

Labs Recommended

- Provoked urine or porphyrin testing. Continued monitoring of urine toxic elements to evaluate benefit.

Support

- Milk thistle, dandelion leaf extract, garlic, cilantro, glutathione, and NAC.

CHLORELLA/CILANTRO

Protocol Details

- Chlorella 3-9 g (total daily dose) given once daily or divided twice daily given 30-60 minutes before meals. Cilantro is given after meals. Low dose, mobilizing dose, and chelating doses will differ.

Benefits

- Best used in combination with each other to potentiate detox. Chlorella is antiviral, increases glutathione, binds to heavy metals, and contains easily absorbed forms of B12 and B6. It is also high in amino acids and can help restore healthy gut flora.

Risks

- Controversial data to support use; must use in combination for effectiveness.

Labs Recommended

- Hair metal, urine, porphyrin, or blood test to evaluate metal burden. Repeat labs to monitor efficacy.

Support

- Milk thistle, dandelion leaf extract, garlic, cilantro, glutathione, NAC.

SPIRULINA

Protocol Details

- Dosed 20-30 g/day starting as low as 500 mg daily, titrating up slowly, working towards a maintenance dose of 3-6 g/day. No specific protocol for length of time for detox.

Benefits

- Immune boosting properties, high in B vitamins, essential elements, calcium, and protein. Spirulina is alkalizing for the body and boosts liver function.

Often taken with chlorella for synergistic detox purposes. May help decrease candida overgrowth.

Risks

- Not as efficient at detoxing heavy metals as well as other products. May cause fever, green stools, gas, restlessness, skin issues, and sleepiness. Contraindicated with seafood or iodine allergies.

Labs Recommended

- Hair metal, urine, porphyrin, or blood test to evaluate metal burden. Repeat labs to monitor efficacy.

Support

- Best if taken with chlorella and liver support such as milk thistle, garlic, and NAC.

ZEOLITE
Protocol Details

- Typically comes in a spray formula. Start with 1 spray once daily and gradually increase to 3 sprays twice daily as tolerated.

Benefits

- Can remove toxic heavy metals, chemicals, VOC's, radioactive toxins, and free radicals (without removing vital nutrients).

Risks

- Very safe, low side effect profile, but lacking in research.

Labs Recommended

- Hair metal, urine, porphyrin, or blood test to evaluate metal burden. Repeat labs to monitor efficacy.

Support

- Milk thistle and NAC. Lower dose temporarily if experiencing die off symptoms.

After supporting and addressing detox, children frequently make gains in eye contact, speech, and awareness, and experience decreased hyperactivity or stimming. In some children, improvement is more subtle. Their sleep may improve, or they might make slight language advances. Patients tend to progress gradually but globally because we've lowered the body burden to give them a better chance for development.[12]

12   J.B. Adams et al., "Safety and Efficacy of Oral DMSA Therapy for Children with Autism
     Spectrum Disorders: Part A--Medical Results," *BMC Clinical Pharmacology*, 9 (2009):
     16; J.B. Adams et al., "Mercury, Lead, and Zinc in Baby Teeth of Children with Autism
     vs. Controls," *Journal of Toxicology and Environmental Health, Part A* 70 (2007): 1046-51;
     J.B. Adams et al, "Toxic Metals and Essential Minerals in the Hair of Children with Autism
     and Their Mothers. *Biological Trace Elements Research* 110 (2006): 193-209; J. Bradstreet et
     al., "A Case-Control Study of Mercury Burden in Children with Autistic Spectrum Disorders,"
     Journal of the American Physicians and Surgeons 8 (2003): 76-79; S.J.S. Flora and G. Saxena,
     "Environmental Occurrence, Health Effects and Management of Lead Poisoning," in *Lead
     Chemistry, Analytical Aspects, Environmental Impacts and Health Effects* (Elsevier: 2013); S.J.S.
     Flora, M. Mittal and A. Mehta, "Heavy Metal Induced Oxidative Stress & Its Possible Reversal
     by Chelation Therapy," *Indian Journal of Medical Research* 128 (2008): 501-23; D.A. Geier
     and M.R. Geier, "A Prospective Assessment of Porphyrins in Autistic Disorders: a Potential
     Marker for Heavy Metal Exposure," *Neurotoxicity Research* 10(2006): 57-64; R. Nataf et
     al., "Porphyrinuria in Childhood Autistic disorder: Implications for Environmental Toxicity,"
     Toxicology and Applied Pharmacology 214 (2006): 99-108; D. A. Geier et al., "Biomarkers of
     Environmental Toxicity and Susceptibility in Autism." *Journal of the Neurological Sciences* 280
     (2009): 101-108; D.E. Stangle et al., "Succimer Chelation Improves Learning, Attention, and
     Arousal Regulation in Lead-exposed Rats but Produces Lasting Cognitive Impairment in the
     Absence of Lead Exposure," *Environmental Health Perspectives* 115 (2007): 201-9.

CHAPTER SEVEN

GENETIC GRIDLOCK

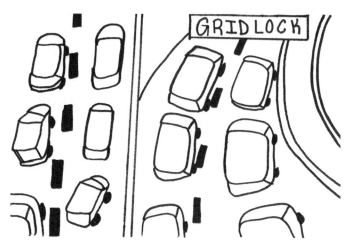

People often think genetics are destiny. That's unfortunate, because it can lead some families to avoid genetic testing, for fear of discovering an unsolvable problem. That puts people in genetic gridlock, when, in reality, genetic testing can reveal many actionable issues, open up exciting alternate routes, and get them moving in the right direction more quickly.

There is so much to discover in the world of genetics. What we normally think of as "genes" is only the tip of the iceberg. As we described in the introduction, looking at genes can be like browsing the books on the library's shelves. All we see is the spines and the covers, yet the important information is held in the words inside. We have to open each book and look carefully at what's within.

There are somewhere around 20,000 genes in the human genome. For each gene, each person gets a code from Dad and a code from Mom. The information is stored in chemical bases called adenine (A), guanine (G), cytosine (C), and thymine (T). Together, these are paired with a sugar molecule and a phosphate molecule that then makes a nucleotide. Nucleotides are then arranged in a specific order to make a gene function optimally. When we have alterations in those genes they're known as single nucleotide polymorphisms or SNPs.[1] For example, if the gene is supposed have two C nucleotides as its wild type (or nonmutated code) and Dad contributes a T but Mom contributes a C, this is called a one-copy, or heterozygous, mutation. If both Dad and Mom donated a T, that would be a double-copy mutation, also known as homozygous. A homozygous mutation can mean more of an impairment within that gene but not always. The SNP is gene specific. Either way, it's a difference, but this doesn't necessarily

---

1   "What is DNA," in *Genetics Home Reference: Your Guide to Understanding Genetic Conditions* (NIH, U.S. National Library of Medicine, 2018) https://ghr.nlm.nih.gov/primer/basics/dna

mean the gene doesn't work 100 percent. It just writes a different story.

The way we explain it to parents is that we must consider genes because they influence the biochemical processes in the body. We typically don't find genetic variations that will cause a change in physical characteristics, which are often found even before the child is born or soon after their birth due to their influence on physical characteristics (like flat noses or low-set ears). We are looking for genes that influence subtleties such as how the patient methylates, detoxes, and makes neurotransmitters.

Since the human genome was mapped in 2003, we know that everybody has SNPs. We see these as individual differences in children, not defects necessarily. Of the 20,000 genes in the body, around 10,000 have been studied, and only about one hundred are well-understood for their role in ASD. (These are gross statistics and change every day.) We encourage families to get testing and work with a functional medicine practitioner to interpret their results. Functional medicine focuses mostly on how we can change our environment to best influence the optimal expression of our genes, a process called epigenetics.

We get excited studying nutrigenomics and discovering how these SNPs may be influencing processes in our patients. SNPs around glutathione genes, for example, might make someone more susceptible to toxic injury because they lack that nutrient essential for detoxification. If we have a child with that mutation, it gives us a clue that we might need to replete glutathione.

We cannot change anybody's genotype. The way we think of it is that genes load the gun and the environment pulls the trigger. The blueprint was written long before the child was born, during mitosis. We can't change that, but we may be able to change how the gene is being expressed or silenced.

When looking at a child on the spectrum genetically, one of our first steps is to make sure they don't have other common variants that can cause autistic-like behaviors, such as Angelman syndrome, Rett Syndrome, or Fragile X. Then we look for SNPs. Within the confines of this book, it would be impossible to discuss all of the possible SNPs and their effects. Instead, we'll concentrate on five categories we commonly focus on: methylation, neurotransmitters, mitochondria, detoxification, and inflammation.

METHYLATION

Methylation is a process of biochemical conversions happening in our bodies, billions of times a second, that is imperative for the proper functioning of almost all of our body systems. With decreased methylation, the body will not be able to execute many important chemical functions in the body. There are many nutrients needed to support this process. The folate pathway, for instance, is incredibly important for methylation. We need folinic acid for growth and development, and methyl folate for neurotransmission, detoxification, energy metabolism, and more.[2]

Another biomarker we look for is the methylenetetrahydrofolate reductase (MTHFR) mutation, which prevents the breakdown of folate into its most active, or methylated, form. Patients with this mutation will have a higher need for methyl folate. We also look at a few other genes as well, such as FOLR1, the folate receptor 1 gene. Patients who have variants in these genes can sometimes benefit from higher doses of folinic acid.[3]

Many people are familiar with a related issue: folic acid has regularly been recommended for expectant mothers since it was discovered that some methylation variants prevent mothers from carrying a baby to term because they can't supply adequate folate. The supplementa-

2   F. El-Baz, "Study of the C677T and 1298AC Polymorphic Genotypes of MTHFR Gene in Autism Spectrum Disorder," *Electronic Physician* 9, no. 9 (September 25, 2017): 5287-93; D. Mischoulon and M.F. Raab, "The Role of Folate in Depression and Dementia," *Journal of Clinical Psychiatry* 68, Suppl. 10 (2007): 28-33.

3   Richard Frye, et al., "The Efficacy of High-Dose Folinic Acid for Autism Spectrum Disorder: A Double-Blind Placebo Controlled Study, " *Molecular Psychiatry* 23 (2018): 247-256.

tion effort is aimed at reducing miscarriages and birth defects.[4]

MTRR AND GIF

Another possibility is SNPs in the B12 genes, the genes needed for regeneration of B12 and pushing B12 into the cells (with the Methyltetrahydrofolate-Homocysteine Methyltransferase Reductase, MTRR, gene). Having a SNP in one of the MTRR genes can inhibit the ability to have adequate B12 intracellularly. It's often not obvious when these patients have a B12 deficiency. They'll have a lot of B12 floating around in their blood, but it's not getting absorbed into the cells, so in fact, their blood levels may look high when, indeed, they are deficient.[5] They may lack gastric intrinsic factor (a GIF mutation), necessary for absorption of B12 in the stomach, which means that oral B12 may not be as effective as a sublingual or injectable form. Taking B12 in high doses isn't a problem because it's water soluble. We urinate out what our bodies aren't able to use.[6]

---

4   L. Luo et al., "Polymorphisms of Genes Involved in the Folate Metabolic Pathway Impact the Occurrence of Unexplained Recurrent Pregnancy Loss," *Reproductive Sciences* 22, no. 7 (2015):845-851.

5   Stephan M. Tanner et al., "Inherited Cobalamin Malabsorption: Mutations in Three Genes Reveal Functional and Ethnic Patterns," *Orphanet Journal of Rare Diseases* 7 (2012): 56.

6   L. Hannibal et al., "Biomarkers and Algorithms for the Diagnosis of Vitamin B12 Deficiency," *Frontiers in Molecular Biosciences* 3 (2016): 27.

NEUROTRANSMITTERS

Three genes related to neurotransmitters that are particularly important to autism are monoamine oxidase A (MAOA), glutamic acid decarboxylase (GAD1), and catechol-O-methyltransferase (COMT).

MAOA

MAOA is an important genotype that helps the body break down serotonin. A variance in this gene is seen in children with autism. These children can be more defiant and oppositional. We can support this variant by giving them an S-adenosyl-L-methionine (SAMe), which is a universal donor to the gene that helps speed up the degradation and absorption of serotonin. Lithium orotate, magnesium, and phenibut also aid in this process. Some people with high levels of B12 in the blood can even benefit from lithium orotate, as it aids with driving B12 into the cell. (This is not to be confused with the lithium used for psychiatric patients with bipolar disorder.)[7]

GAD1

The GAD1 gene helps with the conversion of glutamine to GABA. Glutamate is the excitatory neurotransmitter. It has to be converted to GABA, which is an inhibi-

---

7   V. Ramakrishnan and Akram Husain, "MAOA Gene Associated with Aggressive Behavior in Humans," *Journal of Down Syndrome and Chromosome Abnormalities* 13, no. 1 (2017).

tory neurotransmitter that has a calming effect. If that conversion isn't happening effectively, a child can be overstimulated, hyperactive, and hard to calm down, as well as exhibiting a lot of sleep issues and anxiety. With one or two copies of the GAD1 mutated, we might implement higher doses of magnesium. L-theanine and higher doses of inositol and phenibut (the bioactive form of GABA) are also helpful for reducing glutamate levels and anxiety.[8] Some children benefit from giving GABA directly, but sometimes it can have the opposite effect. Because glutamate conversion is linked to anxiety, a lot of drugs on the market try to block it instead. If we block conversion, we saturate glutamate receptors in children with these GAD1 SNPs, and they experience a sudden calm, lower anxiety, and better sleep. If they're autistic, their stimming often goes down.

Glycine, L-theanine, magnesium, phenibut, and CBD oil can be very helpful for this genetic condition. CBD oil is not marijuana; it's cannibadiol. It's a hemp oil that is legal in all fifty states. It's 0.3 percent or less THC, so this will not get a child "high" or have a psychoactive response. CBD has also been very effective in children with seizures, and now there is even an FDA-approved medication for children with seizures that are treatment

---

8   N.N. Zavadenko and Nlu Suvorinova, "[The Results of the Pharmacological Treatment of Attention Deficit Hyperactivity Disorder: Evaluation with Neuropsychological Methods]," *Zhurnal Nevrologii I Psikhiatrii imeni S.S. Korsakova* 114, no. 9 (2014): 19–24.

resistant.[9] Seizures are so common in autism it makes CBD an appealing compound for some parents. We urge parents to talk to a doctor first about dosage if using it concurrently with seizure meds (as some believe it might inhibit the detoxification of the seizure med, leading to higher, and possibly more toxic, levels of the seizure medication).[10]

COMT

Finally, the last gene we look at is the COMT gene. The COMT gene helps degrade dopamine and catecholamines. Catecholamines are the fight-or-flight compounds: epinephrine, norepinephrine, and dopamine. When the body gets flooded by these catecholamines, the gene helps bring levels down to a more optimal or stable level. Mutations in the COMT gene that are doubly mutated seem to have the most impact on children.[11] The body gets flooded with emotions and the person is likely to stay more "activated" or angry for a longer period of time, possibly needing a longer cool-off period. Other

---

9   "FDA Approves First Drug Comprised of an Active Ingredient Derived from Marijuana to Treat Rare, Severe Forms of Epilepsy," *FDA News Release,* June 25, 2018, https://www.fda.gov/newsevents/newsroom/pressannouncements/ucm611046.htm.

10   Emilio Perucca, "Cannabinoids in the Treatment of Epilepsy: Hard Evidence at Last?" *Journal of Epilepsy Research* 7, no. 2 (2017): 61-76.

11   M.B. Stein et al., "COMT Polymorphisms and Anxiety-Related Personality Traits," *Neuropsychopharmacology* 30, no. 11 (November 2005): 2092-102.

supplements that might be helpful are higher doses of SAMe, omegas, and phosphatidylserine.

On a personal note, figuring out methylation and neurotransmitters can change anyone's life, not just autism patients. By addressing her own methylation pathways, Emily was able to go off antidepressants—medications she was put on in high school and told she would likely need for the rest of her life—completely. Likewise, Jana has some OCD and anxiety issues, but a little bit of inositol and glycine helps her sleep and feel better. It's empowering to realize we can exert more control than we thought over aspects of our mood by knowing their genetic roots. Sometimes, it just requires the correct amount and type of support to see dramatic improvement. Knowing an individual's genetic mutations can help do just that.

MITOCHONDRIA

We've mentioned mitochondria a couple of times in this book, and we're bringing it up again because certain genetic SNPs can throw a wrench in the mitochondrial "energy production factory." Many biochemical reactions have to happen for these organelles to adequately produce that energy, also known as adenosine triphosphate, or ATP, the gas for our brain.

We often talk about this chain of reactions like putting a

quarter in a bubble gum machine. A number of events have to happen between the time we put the coin in the slot and when the gum comes out. That chain of events in mitochondria is very dependent on nutrients like heme, which comes from iron, and essential fatty acids. The fatty acids must make it across the phospholipid layer of fat surrounding the cell to feed the mitochondria. Carnitine provides the ferry. Once the fatty acids cross the lipid layer, the chain reaction starts. The fuels it uses are heme, coenzyme Q10, folate, and more.

Sometimes in that chain of events, we see genetic SNPs that hinder the process. When we test for genetic SNPs, we look at the genes that influence the mitochondrial respiratory chain: COX5A/6C, NDUFS7, UQCRC2, and ATP5G3.

SLC19A1

One of the most important genes in folate delivery is the solute carrier family 19 member 1 (SLC19A1) gene. It's a solute carrier gene that may be more important than those in the respiratory chain because it affects the flow of fuel to the mitochondria, or "gas to the car." Mutations can impede optimal absorption of folate into the body. If a child has multiple methylation SNPs, they may need methylated folate. In our experience, a large majority of children on the spectrum benefit from supporting their mitochondria with nutrients, especially those with underlying mitochondrial SNPs.

A number of studies show these markers of mitochondrial dysfunction in an autistic brain correlating with behaviors in autism. In one, children with autism showed a higher level of oxidative damage to mitochondrial proteins.[12] Oxidative damage means that the body is rusting rather than detoxing free radicals. The more rusting, the more affected the mitochondria.[13] The same study also reported significant decreases in activity of superoxide dismutase 2 (SOD2), a gene in the detox pathway.

For some, repletion of the mitochondrial nutrients can be life-changing, like children with seizures who also have mitochondrial disorders. Repleting these nutrients can be hugely helpful in bringing the seizure threshold down.

Parents need to be aware that it's not just one gene versus another in mitochondrial health, but an accumulation of SNPs in the chain. If somebody has one heterozygous gene, it may not be a big deal for the patient. Multiple instances, on the other hand, can be cause for worry. If they have many variations in the pathways, they likely

---

12 S. Rose et al., "Oxidative Stress Induces Mitochondrial Dysfunction in a Subset of Autistic Lymphoblastoid Cell Lines," *Translational Psychiatry* 1, no. 4 (April 2014): e377.

13 S.J. James, "A Functional Polymorphism in the Reduced Folate Carrier Gene and DNA Hypomethylation in Mothers of Children with Autism," *American Journal of Medical Genetics Part B: Neuropsychiatric Genetics* 153B, no. 6 (September 2010): 1209-20.

have a greater need for nutrient and mitochondrial support. These children can benefit from mito cocktails at higher dosages.

GENES IN THE DETOX PATHWAY

On a long road trip, it pays to stop every once in a while to change the oil so the engine doesn't get clogged up with dirty oil. The same idea applies to the autism journey—the more toxins we can remove from the system, the smoother the "ride" for our patients.

GSTP1

Some children with polymorphisms in their glutathione gene are more susceptible to mercury toxicity and other xenobiotic toxicities. In fact, the glutathione S-transferase pi 1 gene (GSTP1) is probably the biggest player in detoxification. GSTP1 limits the rate at which the body produces glutathione, one of the most powerful antioxidants that binds up toxins in phase one and two of the liver pathways.[14] A lot of children on the spectrum are glutathione deficient, which makes them more vulnerable to injury from lack of detox.

We tell parents that the glutathione cycle works like a dog

---

14   J. Zhang et al., "Pleiotropic Functions of Glutathione S-Transferase P," *Advances in Cancer Research* 122 (2014): 143–75.

chasing its own tail. As these children are likely in a highly stressed state, they're depleting their glutathione very quickly because of inflammation. Tylenol even depletes glutathione because it's detoxified through the liver.[15] (Remember, we advise against giving Tylenol before and after vaccines.)

Glutathione can be given in multiple ways, such as a transdermal cream that is rubbed on the skin or given orally, by rectal suppository, or nebulized and inhaled. It's probably best absorbed via IV, but it can be hard to get children to do that. One challenge with administering glutathione is that it tastes like rotten eggs because it's a sulfur derivative. Taking it orally can be difficult for some children, as can inhalation. The suppository is a great option, as is the cream, although the cream is not as completely absorbed. The great thing about glutathione is that even applying a little bit will yield a wide range of benefits.

SOD2

Another gene in the detox pathway is superoxide dismutase 2 (SOD2). It's an antioxidant enzyme responsible for cleaning up the mitochondria. It protects the brain,

---

15 M. Emmett, "Acetaminophen Toxicity and 5-Oxoproline (Pyroglutamic Acid): A Tale of Two Cycles, One an ATP-Depleting Futile Cycle and the Other a Useful Cycle," *Clinical Journal of the American Society of Nephrology* 9, no. 1 (2014): 191-200.

lungs, and other tissues from oxidative stress.[16] Children with ASD can often have issues with this pathway. A polymorphism in this gene causes a buildup of oxygen free radicals. Antioxidants are especially important for children with these mutations. These antioxidant enzymes are powerful enough to neutralize up to one million free radicals per second. Food sources like green tea and resveratrol, the antioxidant form found in red wine, are also good for this gene. Turmeric is another top antioxidant and has strong evidence for anti-inflammatory properties with autism.[17] Turmeric should have at least 95 % curcuminoids in it. Black pepper extract, sulforaphanes, vitamin C, and vitamin E are also useful supports for the SOD antioxidant pathways.

CTH

Cystathionine gamma-lyase (CTH) is an enzyme which breaks down cystathionine into cysteine, a powerful antioxidant in our body. Active B6, or P5P, is a cofactor of this enzyme. SNPs in this gene can decrease a child's ability to produce glutathione, which we know is a very powerful antioxidant. Cystathionine, which is a gene that

16 H. Van Remmen et al., "Life-Long Reduction in MnSOD Activity Results in Increased DNA Damage and Higher Incidence of Cancer but Does not Accelerate Aging," *Physiological Genomics* 16, no. 1 (December 2003): 29-37.

17 R. Bhandari and A. Kuhad, "Neuropsychopharmacotherapeutic Efficacy of Curcumin in Experimental Paradigm of Autism Spectrum Disorders, *Live Sciences* 141 (November 15, 2015): 156-69.

helps produce the powerful antioxidant known as cysteine, is another antioxidant in the detox pathway worth mentioning.[18] We give these children oral or nebulized n-acetylcysteine and it helps with not only brain inflammatory stress but can also help detox ammonia. Children with PANDAS also appear to do well on NAC. Since it raises glutathione, hospitals use it to rescue people with Tylenol overdoses.

CBS

The CBS gene is one that genetic specialists have differing opinions about. It stands for cystathionine-beta-synthase. The CBS gene is between homocysteine, an important precursor to methylation, and the downstream portion of this detox pathway. It can help rid the body of ammonia and sulphites. If someone has one or two copies of this gene, the worry is that they're not producing enough glutathione. Theoretically, this person's body will deplete homocysteine faster than normal, hindering the transsulfuration pathway. The thing is, it's not a great idea to automatically eliminate some of the foods that can worsen the effects of this mutation, like cruciferous vegetables, onion, garlic, and eggs, because they are some of the healthiest foods available. Before removing these from the diet, we always look at ammonia, taurine, and

---

18   B.D. Paul et al., "Neurodegeneration in Huntington's Disease Involves Loss of Cystathionine y-lyase," *Cell Cycle* 13, no. 16 (August 15, 2014): 2491–93.

urine sulfite levels to identify abnormal amounts in the body. Unless we know the patient can't detoxify ammonia, we don't want them to miss out on excellent sources of important antioxidants.

NAT2

The NAT2, n-acetyltransferase 2, is another obvious detox gene. It helps metabolize certain drugs and chemicals that we use in our daily lives, like perfumes, candles, and cleaning products.[19] People with one or two copies of this gene can seem very chemically sensitive. They process toxins slower and, as a result, have higher incidences of drug toxicity and cancer. The greater the toxicities, the greater the chemical sensitivities are because the body burden is increased. Treatment in this case is more detox support with things like green tea and NRF2 activators, which increase antioxidant support. Milk thistle, pomegranate, berries, and other antioxidant foods help the body break up the toxins so the body can poop, pee, or sweat them out.

It's a lot to consider, but it's crucial to remember to look at the big picture. One gene or polymorphism isn't everything. These aren't Mendelian defects or mutations that absolutely will affect the phenotypic expression of the

---

19 J.A. Agúndez, "Polymorphisms of Human N-Acetyltransferases and Cancer Risk," *Current Drug Metabolism* 9, no. 6 (July 2008): 520–31.

body (the genes the geneticists are focused on treating). Just because someone has a gene, it doesn't mean they will have the absolute worst expression of the gene. It's usually a combination of different genetic variances that cause physiological processes in the body. Focusing on one gene isn't likely to yield much. That's why we ask people to take a step back and get their methylation, detoxification, and mitochondrial health in order.

INFLAMMATION AND GENES

All along this journey, we are always scanning the horizon for inflammation. Some of us have SNPs that turn on the lights of inflammation a little bit quicker. Others can tolerate more. We look to see if the lights of inflammation are coming on prematurely, or if they are not turning off when they should.

Inflammation can be very useful if it's an appropriate immune response to an environmental trigger. If a person skins his or her knee, it's good for the knee to become inflamed so the chemical messengers flood the site and repair it. However, if the body is upregulating all the time because of inflammatory chemicals, that can then trigger an overreaction, or autoimmunity. We want a healthy balance of inflammation within the body. Specific genes can upset this balance.

TNF

Tumor necrosis factor (TNF) is one. It's a cytokine, or inflammatory molecule, that helps with immune cell proliferation, differentiation, and apoptosis. The TNF decides if something coming into the body is harmful or not, and mutations have been associated with various types of cancer. If it identifies the intruder as trouble, it tries to get rid of it.[20] A mutated TNF gene can cause it to misidentify neutral or beneficial input as threatening, thus increasing the risk of inflammation and autoimmune disease state.

FUT2

The fucosyltransferase, or FUT2, is another gene we look at. The FUT2 gene is responsible for producing specific sugars that are secreted into the bowel by intestinal cells. These sugars help attract beneficial bacteria. Mutations in the FUT2 are known as poor secretors. Patients with poor secretors can have lower levels of beneficial bacteria and higher risk of inflammatory bowel disease.[21]

---

20 Ke Ma, Hongxiu Zhang, and Zulgarnain Baloch, "Pathogenetic and Therapeutic Applications of Tumor Necrosis Factor (TNF) in Major Depressive Disorder: A Systematic Review," *International Journal of Molecular Sciences* 17, no. 5 (2016): 733.

21 I. Reguigne-Arnould et al. "Relative Positions of Two Clusters of Human Alpha-L-Fucosyltransferases in 19q (FUT1-FUT2) and 19p (FUT6-FUT3-FUT5) within the Microsatellite Genetic Map of Chromosome 19," *Cytogenetics and Cell Genetics* 71, no. 2 (1995): 158–62.

AOC1

Another gene, diamine oxidase (once known as DAO, now known as amine oxidase, copper containing 1, AOC1) affects the way people process histamines in their food. When a person has one or two copies of the AOC1 gene, it may affect the enzymes that break down those histamines. Children who have two copies of this gene (homozygous) seem to be the ones who need a low histamine diet or use of DAO enzymes. Patients that have a homozygous mutation of this gene (remember, that means it was an abnormal code for the gene passed down from both parents) are more affected clinically. Many foods high in histamines are quite healthful, such as berries, greens, avocados, tomatoes, fish, eggs, and bananas. Children who eat substantial amounts of these foods can have symptoms of high histamines, like migraines, stomach pain, fatigue, or even focus issues. These patients often think they're having an allergic reaction, but that's not really what's happening. Histamines simply aren't getting broken down as they normally would. We tell parents to watch how many histamine foods their child eats and notice if there is any flushing or blotchiness, classic signs. Patients can take a diamine oxidase enzyme to help degrade the histamines, but it's unrealistic to use it with every meal, so we recommend just watching the load. We may also offer quercetin in high doses because it stabilizes the mast cells responsible for histamine release.[22]

---

22   D. Kempuraj et al., "Inhibitory Effect of Quercetin on Tryptase and Inetrleukin-6 Release, and Histidine Decarboxylase mRNA Transcription by Human Mast Cell-1 Cell Line," *Clinical and Experimental Medicine* 6 (2006): 150–56.

VDR

The vitamin D receptor, or VDR SNP, is a gene that can influence the levels of vitamin D in the body.[23] Vitamin D is an anti-inflammatory that acts as a steroid to protect the immune system and prevent long-term illness, even asthma and heart disease. Estimates consider up to 90 percent of Americans to be low in vitamin D. The VDR SNP makes it even harder to pull people up to optimal levels. When we check a patient, we often see vitamin D in the teens or twenties. (Normal ranges are 30-100, but because this hormone is so powerful for so many positive things in the body, we like to see our patients closer to 80-90.) Let's say we give them 10,000 units of vitamin D for two months and check them again. If the vitamin D level only went up to thirty, we will begin to suspect an issue with this gene. This might mean they need year-round supplementation.

The United States government tells us that adults need 600 international units (IU) of vitamin D. If you have a mutation in your VDR gene, it is very likely you will need more (especially to get into the therapeutic ranges discussed above). The heterozygous mutation makes it so that adults likely need 5,000 IU per day. Someone with a homozygous copy may need to take around 10,000 units.

---

23 M. Herdick, A. Steinmeyer and C. Carlberg, "Antagonistic Action of a 25-Carboxylic Ester Analogue of 1Alpha, 25-Dihydroxyvitamin D3 Is Mediated by a Lack of Ligand-Induced Vitamin D Receptor Interaction with Coactivators," *Journal of Biological Chemistry* 275, no. 22 (June 2000):16506-12.

Providers avoid recommending high doses of vitamin D because of the possibility of vitamin D toxicity. Most don't consider that the government guidelines are for people without the VDR SNPs. (We've never seen a vitamin D toxicity case in our careers.)

Vitamin D is not a vitamin as much as it is a hormone. It changes protein function within the body. It's most well-known for its synergistic effect with calcium, bone mineralization and formation. Because vitamin D is "the sunshine vitamin," we recommend every child get out in the sun for twenty minutes a day, preferably with some skin exposed, and barefoot if possible. (People with a naturally dark skin tone have natural sun protection and require at least three to five times longer exposure to make the same amount of vitamin D as a person with a white skin tone. If sunscreen is used, this reduces Vitamin D synthesis by more than 95 percent.)[24] For people with the mutation, however, the sun is not enough. In fact, for the majority of people with VDR mutations, the sun will never be enough, so checking blood levels is critical to ensure optimal supplementation. Vitamin D supplementation can be a powerful anti-inflammatory tool.

---

24   R. Nair and A. Maseeh, "Vitamin D: The 'Sunshine' Vitamin," *Journal of Pharmacology and Pharmacotherapeutics* 3, no. 2 (2012): 118-26.

THE BIG PICTURE

Looking at a child's specific genetic situation is an excellent way to find clues on what's happening in their bodies, but we can't emphasize enough focusing on the big picture. Genetic predisposition is important, but the environmental milieu around the individual is what is most critical. How is the environment influencing the expression of the genes? A lot of the effects of negative genes can be minimized this way.

Everybody has mutations. That's why identical twins can lead completely different lives and get completely different phenotypic expressions (and wind up with different diseases). If one smokes two packs of cigarettes a day and eats fast food often, while the other is a yogi on a Mediterranean diet, one sibling is going to age and die much faster, even with the same genes. It's always been known that environment affects us, but we are just looking at it on a more microscopic and scientific level.

Remember, the gene loads the gun, but the environment pulls the trigger. Create a different environment around a gene. Give more vitamin D to someone with VDR. Give more probiotics for the gut to someone with FUT. Avoid Tylenol if someone has the GSTP1 gene. We follow the genetic signposts that guide us to choose the right supplements.

CONCLUSION

CONTINUING THE JOURNEY

Parents need to remember that treatment is a long-haul road trip, not a weekend jaunt. More of a marathon than a sprint. We applaud parents who are patient with their child's progress. It's often hard to see changes overnight because the body does not process things quickly. Occasionally, some families try a treatment, and the results seem instantaneous. The child wakes up the next day talking for the first time, but that's not usually the case, so we have to be realistic with our expectations. We encourage parents to find a good support network their child can access over time, whether with a practitioner or some other network.

Remember, we are not trying to change what is to be celebrated about the child with autism, their personality or their gifts. We are trying to decrease the physiological load that is weighing them down from being their best selves. Parents need to celebrate every success and be grateful for the incremental gains. Attitude matters. We have seen cases in which one parent is frustrated because their child's autism isn't gone after six months, while the other parent is grateful that she has her sweet child back after behavioral issues subside. That makes a huge difference for the child.

There is no cure-all for autism. Be wary of products or people that claim to offer a panacea. Approach new things with a healthy degree of skepticism but with the will to never stop trying. Know that symptoms can shift over time through a relapse-remitting cycle. A child can be doing great and then hit a bump in the road. With a supportive network in place—a pit crew—he or she can recalibrate and get moving again.

That's seldom as simple as it sounds, which is why we also recommend that parents seek support from each other. Reach out to other parents who are going through the same kinds of things. Practice self-care. Parents need to sleep, exercise, watch their diet, and not neglect mommy-daddy time away from their children. Maintaining a healthy marriage while raising a child on the spectrum can be difficult. Sometimes what's best for the child is for parents to work through the difficulty and get the support they need.

Every parent, whether they have a child on the spectrum or not, needs to come to a point of acceptance that their children are not going to be perfect. No child is. But every child can benefit from being loved for who they are in every stage of development.

Acceptance doesn't mean giving up. It means not living in the "what ifs." It's being okay with where things stand today. It's knowing that applying functional medicine can help a child become the best and healthiest version of themselves.

We see a lot of parents living in fear. They're in a constant state of fight or flight, fear for what's next for their child, fearful that their child won't recover. Children feel that energy too. Parents have to take a deep breath and say it's okay to be where they are at that moment. They need to accept that they can't control everything and know that they are not alone. Parents must have faith in the tools they can use to improve their child's quality of life and development.

We hope people who pick up this book think that this is a great way to start their own journey and learn how to support their child in the best way possible. If they know someone who might benefit from this book, we hope they can pass it along to help someone else discover what biomedical treatment is. In essence, this book is what applying functional medicine and a biomedical approach to autism looks like. We hope people can use it to provide the quality of life and health their children need.

Just as we promised in the beginning of the book, we don't want to leave families who are longing for more here at a dead end. We understand too well that access to providers who are knowledgeable and have experience in biomedical treatments for autism is very limited. We hope to contribute to bridging this gap by offering the autism community more resources through online learning modules, access to functional labs, and pharmaceutical grade supplements. Readers who are ready to continue the journey can find more information on our website, NeuronutritionAssociates.com.

ABOUT THE AUTHORS

EMILY GUTIERREZ received her doctorate from Johns Hopkins University with a focus in translational medicine and integrative health. She is a certified pediatric nurse practitioner, a certified practitioner through the Institute of Functional Medicine, an adjunct faculty member at the Johns Hopkins School of Nursing, and a seasoned speaker, writer, and researcher.

JANA ROSO holds a bachelor's in human development and family sciences, a master's in nursing, and is a certified pediatric nurse practitioner, trained through the Institute of Functional Medicine and the Medical Academy of Pediatric Special Needs. Together, they co-own Neuronutrition Associates, a clinic specializing in children with neurodevelopmental delays and all things functional medicine.

ABOUT THE ILLUSTRATOR

LIBERTY OLETA MITCHELL is an eleven-year-old award-winning artist that attends the Lamar Fine Arts Academy in Austin, Texas. Despite her young age, she has already assembled an impressive portfolio of work using a wide variety of media, including sketching, mixed media, and sculpture. Liberty enjoys the outdoors, her Girl Scout troop, and has a kind and compassionate heart that is the size of Texas.

ACKNOWLEDGMENTS

First, I would like to acknowledge my husband, James, who without his patience and loving support, completion of this book would have been much more challenging. James is also a partner in our practice, working hard behind the scenes, and his contribution to the success of our business has been instrumental. To my wonderful children, Avery and Will, I sincerely appreciate all the times you were patient with me as I dug in and worked weekend after weekend, writing and editing to get this book published. I hope you two always know that despite any of my career accomplishments, you two have always been the biggest gifts of my life. I love you both tremendously and am so grateful to be your mom. To my mother and father, Bill and Linda. Thank you for being two of my biggest cheerleaders in life. Your love and support has been unfaltering and my gratitude is deep and sincere. Last, but certainly not least, thank you to all of my patients that have given me the chance to walk along side you on your journey to better health.

—EMILY GUTIERREZ

I have so much love and gratitude for my family, who has always supported me on this journey, regardless of my never-ending quest to help heal everyone around me. I have an abundance of love for my husband, Stephen, who initially helped me find the path of healing through food. To my children, who have filled me with compassion and motivated me to help take care of others' children. To my patients and their families, who have allowed me to be a part of their healing journey. Most of all, thanks be to God, who has provided me the tools needed to endlessly search for answers for my patients and never give up on helping them.

—JANA ROSO

To the team that helped us realize this dream, thank you Sheila Trask, Mark Chait, and Kayla Sokol. We also thank all of our clinical mentors, such as Kendal Stewart, MD; Alex Carrasco, MD; and Iris Wingrove, MD. Last, we sincerely thank the Institute of Functional Medicine and the Medical Academy of Pediatric Special Needs.

APPENDIX A

RECIPES

PALEO PANCAKES (GLUTEN- AND DAIRY-FREE)
INGREDIENTS

- 1 spotted banana mashed in a bowl
- 1/4 cup nut butter of choice
- 2–3 eggs
- dash of cinnamon and vanilla

INSTRUCTIONS

Mix all ingredients in a bowl and cook on skillet as you would pancake batter.

If you prefer a thicker pancake, you can add 2–3 tablespoons of cassava flour.

AVOCADO BANANA PUDDING (GLUTEN-, DAIRY-, EGG-, AND NUT-FREE)

INGREDIENTS

- 1 very ripe banana with spots on the skin
- 1/2 ripe avocado
- 1 tablespoon cocoa powder
- 1 teaspoon of honey

INSTRUCTIONS

Place all ingredients in a food processor or blender and blend until smooth.

VEGGIE MUFFINS (GLUTEN- AND DAIRY-FREE)

INGREDIENTS

- 1 medium zucchini, grated
- 1 medium carrot, grated
- 1/4 cup frozen peas
- 1/2 cup almond milk
- 1/4 cup plain coconut or almond yogurt
- 1/4 cup avocado oil
- 2 eggs
- 2 cups almond flour
- 3 teaspoons baking powder

INSTRUCTIONS

1. Preheat oven to 350°F.
2. Place the grated zucchini and carrot onto a clean dish towel and squeeze the juice out.
3. Place the zucchini and carrots into a large mixing bowl along with the peas. Add almond milk, yogurt, avocado oil, and egg, and stir until combined.
4. Mix the flour and baking powder together and then slowly add to the wet ingredients. Fold in gently, until just combined.
5. Spray a 12-hole muffin tray with avocado oil or grease with coconut oil. Spoon the mixture, equally, between the 12 muffin sections. Bake for 20–25 minutes.

TIGER NUT WAFFLES (GLUTEN-, DAIRY-, EGG- AND NUT-FREE)

INGREDIENTS

- 3/4 cup tiger nut flour
- 1/2 cup cassava flour
- 1/4 cup arrowroot flour
- 1 teaspoon baking soda
- 1/2 teaspoon cinnamon
- 1/4 teaspoon sea salt
- 1 cup full-fat coconut milk or hemp milk
- 1/4 cup avocado oil
- 3 teaspoons apple cider vinegar
- 1 teaspoon cinnamon
- 1 teaspoon vanilla

INSTRUCTIONS

1. Mix the dry ingredients in one bowl, then add the wet ingredients one at a time to the dry ingredients.
2. Mix well and add your favorite mix-ins (chocolate chips, fruit, nuts) before pouring onto the waffle iron.

OVERNIGHT CHIA OATS (GLUTEN-, DAIRY-, EGG-, AND NUT-FREE)

INGREDIENTS

- 1/2 cup gluten-free ground or rolled oats
- 1/2 tablespoon hemp seeds
- 1 tablespoon chia seeds
- 1 tablespoon flax seed
- 1/4 cup fresh fruit of choice
- 1/2 ripe banana smashed
- 1/2 cup of hemp milk

INSTRUCTIONS

1. Combine all ingredients into mason jar, screw lid on tight, and shake gently.
2. Place in fridge and enjoy in the morning!

KOMBUCHA POPSICLES (GLUTEN-, DAIRY-, EGG-, AND NUT-FREE)

INGREDIENTS

- 1 1/2 cups kombucha of choice
- 1 cup frozen fruit of choice

INSTRUCTIONS

1. Blend fruit in blender until smooth.
2. Slowly add kombucha and stir with spoon to reach desired consistency.
3. Add to popsicle molds and let freeze overnight.

APPENDIX B

AUTISM RESOURCES

- Neuronutrition Associates
- The Medical Academy of Pediatric Special Needs
- The Institute of Functional Medicine
- Talk About Curing Autism, TACA
- Epidemic Answers
- Documenting Hope
- Generation Rescue
- Our Kids ASD

Made in the USA
Coppell, TX
07 April 2023

15357380R00114